CITYSPOTS
VILNIU

Andrew Quested & Jeroen van Marle

Written by Andrew Quested & Jeroen van Marle

Published by Thomas Cook Publishing
A division of Thomas Cook Tour Operations Limited
Company registration No: 1450464 England
The Thomas Cook Business Park, 9 Coningsby Road
Peterborough PE3 8SB, United Kingdom
Email: books@thomascook.com, Tel: +44 (0)1733 416477
www.thomascookpublishing.com

Produced by The Content Works Ltd
Aston Court, Kingsmead Business Park, Frederick Place
High Wycombe, Bucks HP11 1LA
www.thecontentworks.com

Series design based on an original concept by Studio 183 Limited

ISBN: 978-1-84157-941-2

First edition © 2006 Thomas Cook Publishing
This second edition © 2008 Thomas Cook Publishing
Text © Thomas Cook Publishing
Maps © Thomas Cook Publishing/PCGraphics (UK) Limited
Transport map © Communicarta Limited

Series Editor: Kelly Anne Pipes
Project Editor: Linda Bass
Production/DTP: Steven Collins

Printed and bound in Spain by GraphyCems

Cover photography (National Museum of Lithuania) © Jon Hicks/Alamy

CONTENTS

SYMBOLS KEY

The following symbols are used throughout this book:

ⓐ address ⓣ telephone ⓦ website address ⓔ email
ⓛ opening times ⓝ public transport connections

The following symbols are used on the maps:

i information office		▨ points of interest	
✈ airport		○ city	
✚ hospital		○ large town	
▤ bus station		○ small town	
▤ railway station		═ motorway	
✝ cathedral		━ main road	
❶ numbers denote		━ minor road	
featured cafés & restaurants		━ railway	

Hotels and restaurants are graded by approximate price as follows:
£ budget price **££** mid-range price **£££** expensive

ⓞ *Vilnius's skyline*

INTRODUCING
Vilnius

Introduction

Vilnius, capital of Lithuania, will seduce you in a way that few other cities can. It's a city on a human scale, with an uncanny ability to capture hearts. It doesn't conform to expectations, wriggles free of the confines of any headline and refuses to be slotted into any particular category. But although not many visitors can put their finger on the main attraction, they return time and again. The city's reputation is growing by the day and it's set to become one of the most popular destinations in the Baltic region. Now is the time to visit.

Perhaps, in fact, the appeal lies in Vilnius's lack of main attraction. There's an architectural and historical tapestry of different styles and stories, sights, sounds and smells, that can't be caught in a single image. But the experience as a whole will gently seep into your senses while you're here and then refuse to leave when you do. Whether you're a backpacker or taking a short break in one of Vilnius's eclectic hotels, you'll find plenty to explore during your visit.

History is raw and recent in Lithuania. Vilnius retains a sense of this, both in its architecture and in the customs of its residents. At one time the capital of a regional superpower, at other times fallen victim to a variety of conquerors, the city's buildings display a mishmash of disparate influences from both East and West. And the architectural landscape is still changing fast, as investment fuelled by EU membership starts to make its mark. Old buildings are being restored and shiny new ones thrown up all over town. Nestled among a confusing array of cobbled streets and an abundance of small churches, the new buildings give you a sense of history still in the making.

Lithuanians are as varied a race as the buildings among which they live. You'll see characters of all sorts either strutting confidently down the street or ambling aimlessly around the alleyways and courtyards. Young, trendy students with all-night party habits intermingle with older residents keen to retain their traditions. Join in with the locals, try their food and favourite drinks and adopt their lifestyle for your visit – you'll learn a whole lot more by doing this than by visiting all the museums in the land.

● *The cathedral is one of Vilnius's major attractions*

When to go

SEASONS & CLIMATE

June and July are the warmest months, but they are also peak tourist season, so expect higher prices and longer queues. July is also the wettest month of the year and you can find yourself running for cover from a sudden downpour.

The best time to visit Vilnius is spring or autumn — both of which offer explosions of colour, pleasant weather, fewer tourists, and the bustle of a thriving city.

Winters are for the hardy: temperatures occasionally drop below -20°C (-4°F) and days are short and often cloudy. The cold, however, does offer its own appeal. With several layers of clothing you can enjoy crunching the snow in Vilnius's parks, ice-fishing and walking on frozen lakes, or simply listening to the constant warlike rumble of a flowing yet frozen river. Cross-country skiing is also popular with locals.

ANNUAL EVENTS

There is always something going on in Vilnius. Festivals are a mix of pagan and Christian traditions. Christian calendar highlights including Easter (Velykos) and Shrovetide (Užgavėnės) occur between — or sometimes coincide with — more pagan, nature-inspired events such as the end of winter or midsummer. You're as likely to see masks, decorations made from twigs and grass and burning wicker people as you are to see crosses, Christian robes and a nativity scene. The city often erects a stage in Cathedral Square for concerts and celebrations.

● *A hot-air balloon drifts past the Gothic St Anne's church*

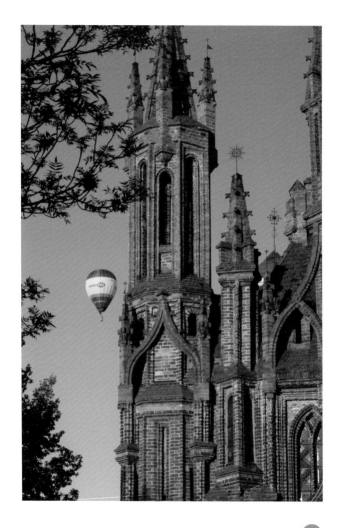

Political and historical events are well celebrated, if in a rather haphazard fashion. Advance planning and publicity are not strong points. Some details of forthcoming events can be found on the Entertainment Bank website (ⓦ www.eb.lt) but it's best to visit the tourist office as soon as you arrive to find out what's happening.

Apart from Kaziukas Fair in March (see page 14) there are three regular annual events that are definitely worth aiming for.

Užgavėnės (Shrovetide), 28 February

Shrovetide or Pancake Day, Užgavėnės in Lithuanian, is one of the wildest of Vilnius's annual celebrations. On Shrovetide itself or the weekend closest to it, locals dress head to foot in costumes and impressive masks based on anything from storks to goats to horses. There are mock fights between costumed characters, snowball throwing, singing and chanting – all culminating in the burning of a huge wicker woman. Most of the activities will take place in front of the Town Hall or in Cathedral Square, although you could cop a snowball in the back of the head anywhere.

Joninės (Midsummer), 23 June

This is a good example of a pagan festival that has taken on a Christian meaning. The national holiday, also known as Rasų, Cupola and Dew, celebrates the longest day and shortest night of the year. Midsummer Day has been identified as St John's Day, although there's actually nothing Christian about the way it is celebrated here.

Traditionally, girls braid wreaths for themselves from field grass and flowers and then, at midnight, take them off and set them afloat in the river. Girls who are in relationships but are not yet married set two wreaths floating off together. If they stay together, they will marry their beloved, whereas if the wreaths float apart, they will split up. 'He loves me, he loves me not' petal-pinching games are also popular.

⬥ *There is a strong folk culture in Lithuania*

● *Wearing a floral wreath for Joninės*

Close to midnight a huge fire is lit and rafts are set alight and sent floating down the river. Pick a good spot on a bridge at midnight – the Baltasis Tiltas (White Bridge) is good for this – and take your camera.

If you really want to get involved in the biggest Joninės celebration, head for the town of Kernavė, about 50 km (31 miles) west of Vilnius. Things tend to be very pagan here, and you'll feel like you've travelled back in time as hessian-clad hippies sing, dance, drink mead and set fire to objects around them — all with birds' nests on their heads.

Kernavė Live Archaeology Festival, early July
Kernavė also hosts an annual Live Archaeology Festival, sometimes called Days of Living History. Here you can experience life pretty much as it would have been in ancient times: you can hack pieces off a flame-grilled pig, sit in a tepee made of twigs, try out old-style archery and watch knights in armour battling it out with sticks and maces. The festival normally takes place a couple of weeks after Joninės, in early July. ⓦ www.kernave.org

Public holidays do not affect visitors to a great extent as most shops and restaurants remain open, except on Christmas Day. Transport runs every day, but weekends and public holidays have a reduced schedule.

PUBLIC HOLIDAYS
New Year's Day & National Flag Day 1 Jan
Independence Day 16 Feb
Restoration of Independence Day 11 Mar
Easter Sunday 23 Mar 2008; 12 Apr 2009
Workers' Holiday 1 May
Joninės (Midsummer) 23 June
Crowning of Mindaugas 6 July
Žolinė (Assumption) 15 Aug
All Saints' Day 1 Nov
Christmas Day 25 Dec

Kaziukas Fair

While still dressed in coats of white snow, Vilnius explodes with colour on the first weekend in March as craftsmen flood in from all over the country to sell their wares at Kaziukas Mugė, St Casimir's Fair.

As with many celebrations in Lithuania the festival's links to Christianity are mingled with an old pagan celebration of the end of winter. St Casimir is the patron saint of Lithuania. He died on 4 March, the time of year when people emerged from hibernation to trade the whittled wooden spoons, woven baskets and dried flower creations they had been working on all winter. March was a good time for travelling and trading, as it was both warm enough to go outside, and cold enough to leave a blanket of snow to drag a sleigh over.

The fair lasts all weekend and, although you don't see too many horses dragging sleighs any more, a good portion of the city is given over to the market. The theme is more or less floral, with *verba* – sticks decorated with dried flowers and grasses from the previous summer – on sale just about everywhere.

In pagan tradition, *verba* had powers of life, health, disease prevention as well as the more practical purpose of making a home smell nicer. Houses were decorated with the colourful floral sticks and people would playfully strike each other on the shoulders and head with them. After Christianity came to Lithuania, *verba* would also be carried to church on Palm Sunday (*Verbų Sekmadienis*) instead of palm leaves.

You'll also have the opportunity to pick up hand-woven baskets, whittled wooden spoons and other utensils, ironwork, ceramics, and all manner of special, hand-made goods. Woodwork and basketwork are particularly popular. Some of the creations you will find on the many stalls are stunning despite their often obscure purpose.

Kaziukas is not only an experience for the colour, hustle and bustle of the market, and the beautiful *verba* that abound. There is also a special feeling of celebration in the air as winter is coming to a close. It's a good example of the mix of pagan and Christian traditions that are now so much a part of Lithuanian culture.

⬤ *Vilnius takes to the streets for the Kaziukas Fair*

History

The region where Lithuania now lies was once covered by a glacier, and when the glacier receded, the first inhabitants to move in were reindeer. Hunting tribes were not far behind them, arriving as early as the 7th century BC. Vilnius itself first came into being in the 11th century when a wooden castle was built on Gediminas Hill to overlook a small settlement below.

Lithuania's first King, Mindaugas, was crowned in 1253 and was responsible for introducing Christianity to Lithuania. He established the cathedral in Vilnius, but most of the population were not impressed. They accepted the new religion's existence but carried on with their pagan traditions of worshipping the sun, tending fires, dancing in the woods and paying homage to nature.

There followed one of Lithuania's most influential periods in history, when Vilnius found itself at the head of a huge regional superpower stretching southeast as far as the Black Sea. In 1323 Grand Duke Gediminas invited foreigners to settle in Vilnius with the promise of religious freedom, and later formed a union with Poland by marrying his daughter, Aldona, to the son of the then Polish king. These two moves combined to create a strong Lithuanian Polish kingdom, which flourished and expanded for the next two centuries. Teutonic knights attacked in 1410 but were defeated in the battle of Žalgiris, also known as Tannenberg.

In the 16th century, however, the Lithuanian Polish dynasty faltered. Polish became the official state language of the region and wars with Russia and Sweden further weakened Lithuania. In 1795, Russia seized Vilnius and all but the most western parts of the country. The Russian occupation lasted 120 years, interrupted only by Napoleon and his army on their ill-fated campaign to Moscow in 1812.

The Russian occupation continued until the Germans arrived to take their place in World War I. Soon after independence was declared in 1918, however, Vilnius was attacked by Poland, which was under the impression that it belonged to them. Lithuania managed to remain independent until 1926, when Hitler and Stalin carved up Europe under the Molotov-Ribbentropp Pact. As a result, almost all Lithuanian Jews were summarily executed and hordes of other Lithuanians found themselves being sent off to Siberia. Lithuanian partisans fled to the forest and waged guerrilla-style warfare against the Soviet occupation. The West turned their backs and ignored their pleas for help.

As the Soviet Union started to crumble, Lithuania declared independence again in 1990. The Soviets did not listen, however, and in 1991 Soviet forces attempted to storm the Lithuanian parliament and TV tower. Thirteen unarmed Lithuanian civilians were killed – a tiny number compared to the hundreds of thousands that had died in the previous years – but the event had much greater symbolic significance. This time the world took notice, and before long Soviet statues were being pulled down all over Lithuania.

Steady independence has given Lithuania a springboard for development and the country's future will hopefully be happier than its past. The country reintroduced its own currency, competed under its own flag at the Winter Olympics in 1992 and joined the European Union and NATO in 2004. Since January 1, 2008 it has been a member of the Schengen Agreement.

Lifestyle

Life can be tough for many Lithuanians, but despite this, they certainly know how to have a good time. Theatres and concert halls are regularly packed, and Vilnius's bars and restaurants are almost always buzzing. Lithuanians like to eat, drink and be merry and – contrary to the Russian cliché – enjoy their excellent local beers as much as a shot of vodka.

Vilnius's large student population means that bars and nightclubs are often open all week and tend not to close until as late as 05.00 or 06.00 at weekends. While there are always plenty of places to have a drink in the evening, nightclubs don't fire up until after 23.00. Certainly, Vilnius is a city that seldom sleeps, particularly in summer.

While Vilnius is far from the bargain it once was due to steadily rising prices, it can still be moderately cheap for Western tourists. Living in Lithuania on a local wage is increasingly tough, however, and you should bear this in mind when taxi drivers or restaurant owners try to charge over the odds. Be clear about rates before accepting a ride or booking a service – the tourist information centre should be able to give you up-to-date advice on reasonable prices to expect.

Cultural differences are something to be aware of. Lithuanians tend to be reserved and quiet, but are friendly, genuine and humble once you break the ice. They seem to welcome similar qualities in visitors. However, concepts of personal space and politeness don't match with those in the West. People tend to queue uncomfortably close to one another to avoid people pushing in, so be prepared for this and don't be afraid to stand your ground. When passing people who are blocking doors or corridors, a quick shove is as normal as a polite 'excuse me' and will often have much more success. Rather than simple rudeness, put this down to local habits – watch what others do and get ready to join in.

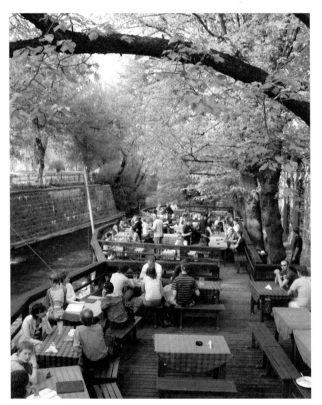

⬤ *Relaxing by the water's edge*

Culture

Vilnius may be small, but it's packed full of cultural attractions. This is partly because of its rich and complex history. Arts were well funded during Soviet times and standards of education and training in this field were high. As a result, you'll find that theatre, music and dance here are at least as good as in much bigger capitals. The city's location on the crossroads between East and West has also helped. Artists from all corners of the world come regularly to Vilnius, providing a wealth of cultural experiences for visitors.

Performance arts – opera, music, drama – are the main cultural highlights of Vilnius, although there are several worthwhile museums in the city. Be aware, however, that live performances are rare during summer, as most locals take their holidays in this period. Museums can also adopt some irregular opening hours.

A good source of information on museums in Vilnius and Lithuania can be found on ⓦ www.muziejai.lt. Most museums and galleries charge a small admission fee, usually under 5Lt.

Before you even think of going to a museum, or to the opera or theatre, keep in mind that there are some fascinating cultural titbits scattered about in the streets. To some extent, Vilnius is a city of secrets. You could be right next to something of note, but not realise until someone points it out or tells you the story behind it. It's also possible to find quaint courtyards or attractive buildings tucked away behind seemingly run-down areas of town.

A guided tour by a knowledgeable local will certainly enhance your cultural experience of the city. The tourist information offices (see page 153) offer regular, good quality – if a little theatrical – tours.

❍ *Vilnius on a winter's day*

● *Traditional dance performance*

As well as the standard walking tours of the city, you can join in a traditional feast (slice-your-own hog roast using a lettuce leaf as a plate, washed down by medieval mead from a clay tusk) or spend an evening watching and learning traditional dances.

Regular tours generally leave from the cathedral (see page 62) at 10.00 and 15.00, but it's best to check times in advance. If you are interested in a particular subject area, such as art, religion, graffiti, ghosts or legends, ask at the tourist information offices about hiring a private guide.

● *Churches and rooftops in Vilnius*

Shopping

Vilnius is not a shopping destination or even, nowadays, a hive of bargains. Shopping here is definitely, however, a worthwhile experience, particularly in the old-fashioned markets and the snakeskin-boots-n-bling shops.

One of the most fun markets is perched on the top of Tauras Hill, in and around the Trade Union Palace. On Saturday mornings the area is filled with stalls offering military memorabilia, collectables including stamps, badges and coins, and assorted antiques that could make interesting souvenirs.

You'll find most of these sellers and more at the eastern edge of the mainstream Kalvarijų Market (see page 98), held just outside of

AMBER – OR TOFFEE?
When buying amber take special care that you are buying the genuine product. Mosaics made of hundreds of little chips of 'amber' have been known to melt and dribble down the wall when hung in direct sunlight – because in fact, they're not made of amber at all but of toffee. You can test amber by sniffing or tasting it (it shouldn't be sweet or plasticky) or by burning it (real amber, when burned, smells like pine-scented air freshener). Most sellers will object to you trying either method. Sugar can be discreetly spotted with a damp finger, but a good guide is the price – you get what you pay for. Try to buy from reputable amber shops rather than street-side stalls.

▶ *Shopping in Vilnius has changed dramatically since Soviet days*

the centre every morning except Monday. You may be able to seek out a bargain from the collection of items for sale – anything from goldfish to second-hand boots to electronics and fake brand names. Whatever you buy, you can carry it with dignity by giving one of the old lady sellers a few coins in return for a plastic shopping bag from an expensive fashion store.

Near the train station is the bustling **Halės Food Market** (ⓐ Pylimo & Bazilijonų ⓛ Early–13.00) selling all manner of produce. It's a fascinating experience for the gourmand as well as an eye-opener for anyone used to supermarkets. If you do want a supermarket, look out for Iki, Maxima and Rimi stores dotted about the city.

🔺 *Market day in Gedimino Prospektas*

USEFUL SHOPPING PHRASES

What time do the shops open/close?
Kada atidaromos/uždaromos/parduotuvės?
Kah-dah ah-teeh-dah-roh-mohs/uzh-darr-om-oss/pahr-dot-oov-ess?

How much is this?
Kiek šitas kainuoja?
Keck sheetus kay-noh-ya?

Can I try this on?
Ar galima pasimatuoti?
Ur gull-im-uh pass-im-ah-totee?

My size is ...
Mano numeris ...
Mah-noh noo-mer-iss ...

I'll take this one, thank you
Aš šitą paimsiu. Ačiū
Ash sheet-ah pah-im-soo. Ah-choo

This is too large/too small/too expensive. Do you have any others?
Per didelis/per mažas/per brangus. Ar turite kà kitų?
Perr did-el-iss/perr mazh-us/perr bran-goose. Ar toor-it-teh kah ki-too?

Iki is the higher quality option, selling a good range of otherwise hard-to-find goods.

There are several modern shopping centres. Gedimino Prospektas is the main drag, with some interesting shops tucked all the way down the western end. The most recent addition, Vilniaus Vartai or 'Gates of Vilnius' (see page 98), features the latest flurry of designer shops. Europa (see page 96) is modern but fairly small and predictable. For a greater range and a better time, try Akropolis (see page 96) which has an ice rink in the centre.

Eating & drinking

Lithuanians traditionally like real hearty man-food: meat and potatoes. Local food is simple but fresh and tasty, and generally of good value. A typical lunchtime meal is battered or fried meat such as pork or chicken, boiled potatoes, and a 'white salad' of more potatoes, peas and carrots in mayonnaise. Coleslaw is often served as an accompaniment.

The Lithuanian national dish is *cepelinai*, or 'zeppelins'. Probably originating in Germany, *cepelinai* are round dumplings made of grated potato wrapped around a piece of spiced meat or curd. They are normally served with a sauce, and the type of sauce reflects the different regional variations of the dish.

Vederai are another traditional variation on the theme of meat and potatoes, consisting of a grilled sheep's intestine filled with creamy mashed potato. Think of it as a potato sausage, as it tastes a lot better than it sounds. You'll find these dishes on offer in many restaurants and they tend to be the best-value option. They're certainly a good way of keeping warm in cold weather. International food is also widely available and of generally good quality, but tends to be more expensive than the local favourites.

Lithuanians enjoy a drink, particularly beer, and will proudly remind you that the local brews often win medals and accolades

PRICE CATEGORIES
Based on the average price of a three-course meal without drinks.
£ up to 15Lt   ££ 15–25Lt   £££ over 25Lt

◆ *Enjoy a drink while watching Vilnius life go by*

USEFUL DINING PHRASES

I would like a table for ... people
Norėčiau staliuko ... Žmonėms
Norr-etch-ow stah-lyoo-koh ... zhmo-nems

May I have the bill, please?	**Waiter/waitress!**
Ar galite atnešti sàskaità?	Padavėjau! Padavėja!
Ur gull-i-teh at-nesh-tee sass-kay-tah?	*Pah-dah-veh-yau! Pah-dah-veh-yah!*

Could I have it well-cooked/medium/rare, please?
Ar galite iškepti visiškai/vidutiniškai/su krauju?
Ur gull-it-eh ish-kept-ee wee-seesh-kay/wee-doo-teenie-shkay/soo crow-yoo?

I am a vegetarian. Does this contain meat?
Aš vegetaras. Ar tai su mėsa?
Ash veh-geh-tah-rahs. Ahr tay suh meh-sah?

Where is the toilet please?
Kur yra tualetas?
Coor ee-ruh too-al-ett-us?

I would like a cup of/two cups of/another coffee/tea
Prašom puodel /du puodelius/dar kavos/arbatos
Prash-om poh-deh-lee/doo poh-deh-loos/dahr kah-voss/ar-bat-oss

in international competitions. The beer tends to be light, crisp, and easy to drink. Be wary, though, as although the beer may look light, its alcoholic content is not. Soak it up with some *užkandžiai prie alaus,* popular beer snacks including *kepinta duona,* little sticks of fried dark bread covered with melted cheese or garlic. For the more adventurous, there are pigs' ears.

In both restaurants and bars, tipping is not required but is a reward for good service. Rounding up your bill to avoid small change or offering an extra ten per cent or so is standard.

Smoking is not permitted in any restaurants, cafés, bars, clubs or other public places. There are one or two places that have a special smoking room, but these are rare.

The whole restaurant scene takes on a different atmosphere in summer, when dozens of outdoor cafés and eateries appear, seemingly from nowhere, and fill streets and courtyards alike. Each of these is attached to a bricks-and-mortar venue, although it can be hard to tell which belongs to which. It's very relaxing to sit outside with a beer or coffee, people-watching until the late evening in summer.

Picnicking is not common among Lithuanians but there's nothing to stop you stocking up at a food market or supermarket (see page 26) and heading for a local park or bench. Locals tend to eat al fresco only out of town, setting up barbecues for friends and family around one of the country's many lakes.

Entertainment & nightlife

One of the great joys of Vilnius is the quality and variety of performances that you can see without making a dent in your holiday budget. Lithuanians, despite what you may think from the Eurovision Song Contest, place a strong emphasis on music and theatre and are proud to show off the excellent results.

In addition, touring artists often turn up in Vilnius and you can sometimes catch big-name international acts without the astronomical ticket prices that you would pay at home. Older heavy metal and rock acts often appear here and the arena in which they play is jokingly called the 'graveyard'.

Theatre is varied and always of good quality, but is generally only performed in Lithuanian. Despite this, the creativity and energy can still make this a moving experience.

For information on upcoming performances, see Ⓦ www.eb.lt. Tickets can generally be purchased at the venue on the evening of the performance, or booked in advance via the theatre's website. There is also a ticket booth in the public square opposite the Novotel Hotel on Gedimino Prospektas.

In warmer months – May to August – you can also come across excellent free music and dance in public spaces. Keep an eye on Cathedral Square, Town Hall Square, and the larger Old Town courtyards, especially on public holidays and festival days. Chances are you'll come across some traditional Lithuanian performances, which can be a real treat. If you happen to be in town in the week before Christmas, you'll find many churches put on free, atmospheric concerts.

A more recent Lithuanian tradition is clubbing until dawn, in one of Vilnius's many eclectic late-night bars and nightclubs.

If you're going out on the town for a spot of late-night dancing, a favourite pastime of young Lithuanians, note that admission to some nightclubs can be as high as 60Lt depending on the venue and night.

🔺 *There's a wide choice of bars and clubs*

Sport & relaxation

SPECTATOR SPORTS

Basketball is like a second religion in Lithuania. The Vilnius team is Lietuvos Rytas, and a game between them and their sworn rivals Žalgiris (from Kaunas) is the Lithuanian equivalent of Real Madrid versus FC Barcelona in Spain. Indeed, it's such an event that Lithuania's borders have been known to close when a game this big is on. See ⓦ www.lkl.lt for local league information.

The biggest games are played at **Siemens Arena** (ⓐ Ozo 14, ⓣ 5247 7550 ⓝ Bus: 53 to Pramogų Arena). For information on games and to book on-line see ⓦ www.bilietai.lt. Schedules and tickets are also available from **Tiketa** (ⓦ www.tiketa.lt).

Even if you can't make it to a game, watching it live in any bar or club in Vilnius is also a great experience – especially if the Vilnius team wins. Be careful not to antagonise any locals if they don't win, however, as there have been reports of some nasty scenes during the European Basketball Championships and other major international competitions in which Lithuania competes.

Football is also played, but is by no measure as popular as basketball.

PARTICIPATION SPORTS

Lithuania is a land of lakes and rivers, so canoeing and kayaking are popular. You can even combine this with camping for a pleasant and quite unique holiday. It's best to go through a specialised tour agency such as **Active Holidays** (ⓣ 6982 4795 ⓦ www.activeholidays.lt).

RELAXATION

A pampering must are a sauna and spa. Most good hotels in town have their own facilities that can be booked by the hour, usually at a special rate for guests. Three of the best are at the CityPark Hotel (see page 39), Radisson (see page 40) and Narutis (see page 39).

Another option is to head out of town to a sauna and spa in a village, which can be delightful, especially in winter when you can combine it with jumping about in the snow or plunging through a hole in a frozen lake. You can add local flavour by asking to be whacked by a leafy birch branch (*vanotis vantom*) or by requesting a honey massage (*masažas su medumi*). Ask one of the tourist information offices to recommend a spa that is currently active in Trakai or Molėtai. If you want to stay overnight, head over to Druskininkai (see page 112).

Be sure when you are booking a sauna that it is clear exactly what you want. If you are quoted what seems like an exorbitantly high price, you are probably being offered 'company', not just the use of the sauna.

⬤ *Basketball is enjoyed by Lithuanians of all ages*

Accommodation

There is a good range of hotels in Vilnius, covering everything with the exception of the high end of the market. There are certainly hotels that lay on the luxury and offer a good-value treat, but there are also more cosy affairs that have plenty of charm without the high prices. Self-catering apartments and B&B-style accommodation are also available, offering excellent value if you prefer to be a bit more independent. Budget travellers can choose from a small selection of basic hostels with, generally, a fun and friendly atmosphere.

The bigger hotels accept bookings on-line, while some of the smaller places, including apartments and B&Bs, will accept email enquiries and faxes. Out of the summer season you can often find accommodation just by turning up without a reservation, but with Vilnius's growing popularity it's always best to book.

HOTELS
Shakespeare Boutique Hotel ££ Vilnius's best-known boutique hotel, tucked away in a quiet backstreet but near Cathedral Square. Rooms are themed on famous authors and literary characters. The unique décor and friendliness of the staff offer a home-away-from-home

PRICE CATEGORIES
Based on the average price of a double room for one night.
£ up to 150Lt   **££** 150–400Lt   **£££** over 400Lt

● *The Stikliai hotel is one of the most refined in Vilnius*

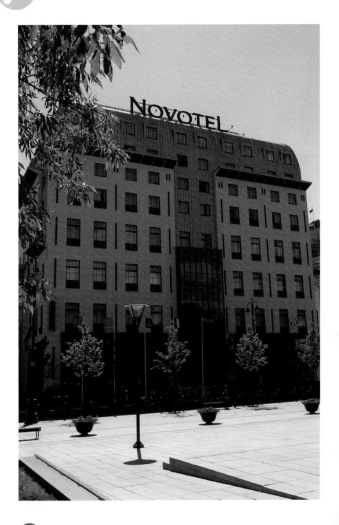

atmosphere. ⓐ Bernardinų 8/8 ⓣ 5266 5885 ⓦ www.shakespeare.lt
Ⓝ Bus: 10, 11, 33 to Dailės Akademija

Atrium £££ The Atrium offers large rooms, clean and simple yet
with all the luxuries you want, including leather furniture, wireless
phones and large-screen televisions. The location near Castle Hill
and the cathedral is excellent, as is the Argentinean-style steak
restaurant. ⓐ Pilies 10 ⓣ 5210 7777 ⓦ www.atrium.lt Ⓝ Bus: 10, 11, 33
to Sereikiškių

CityPark £££ On the corner of Cathedral Square, this large
but homely hotel has one of the widest range of facilities and
room choices around. Don't miss the spa and sauna facilities
hidden away downstairs. ⓐ Stuokos-Gucevičiaus 3 ⓣ 5210 7461
ⓦ www.citypark.lt Ⓝ Bus: 33 to Arkikatedra; 11 to Gedimino

Europa Royale Vilnius £££ An ostentatious and opulent hideaway
decorated by Italian designers. The standard rooms are more
subdued but in any case service is excellent. ⓐ Aušros Vartų 6
ⓣ 5266 0770 ⓦ www.groupeuropa.com Ⓝ Bus: 4, 11, 13, 31, 34, 74;
trolleybus: 1, 2, 5, 7 to Rūdninkų

Narutis £££ You're really getting something special here, and
not just due to the outstanding location. Rooms have all been
individually decorated by a French designer, with frescoes and
original elements of the 16th-century building exposed. ⓐ Pilies 24
ⓣ 5212 2894 ⓦ www.narutis.com Ⓝ Bus: 10, 11, 33 to Sereikiškių

◔ *Some of the best rooms in Vilnius are in the Novotel hotel*

Novotel £££ One of the least attractive buildings in the Old Town but with some of the finest rooms, many with great views. Décor is fairly minimalist, but both the hotel and the rooms have everything you need including free Wi-Fi. One room is set aside for guests with disabilities. ⓐ Gedimino 16 ⓣ 5266 6200 ⓦ www.novotel.com ⓝ Bus: 26, 43, 53; trolleybus: 2, 3, 5, 6, 12, 14 to Vilniaus

Radisson SAS Astorija £££ Charming building with rather strict, square but comfortable and clean rooms. The location right behind the Town Hall is excellent. George W Bush once stayed here. Free Wi-Fi. ⓐ Didžioji 35/2 ⓣ 5212 0110 ⓦ www.vilnius.radissonsas.com ⓝ Bus: 4, 11, 13, 31, 34, 74; trolleybus: 1, 2, 5, 7 to Rūdninkų

Ramada £££ Italian-style décor with a modern twist – gilded furniture, marble-topped tables and flat-screen televisions and DVD players in all rooms. Free Wi-Fi or LAN internet access. ⓐ Subačiaus 2 ⓣ 5255 3355 ⓝ Bus: 4, 11, 13, 31, 34, 74; trolleybus: 1, 2, 5, 7 to Rūdninkų

Stikliai £££ Near the university and exquisite in every respect, with a very refined but charming Mediterranean feel. It's a hotel you stay in to impress and a favourite with visiting VIPs. ⓐ Gaono 7 ⓣ 5264 9595 ⓦ www.stikliaihotel.lt ⓝ Bus: 11 to Vokiečių

APARTMENTS & B&Bs
Litinterp £–££ This long-standing, reputable B&B booking service is the best way to find basic, comfortable accommodation without denting your budget. They also offer home-stay accommodation and a range of other travel services. ⓐ Bernardinų 7–2 ⓣ 5212 3850 ⓦ www.litinterp.com ⓝ Bus: 10, 11, 33 to Daliės Akademija

Veronica B&B £–££ Despite its location on one of the busiest streets in the Old Town, this B&B's courtyard location and live-in hosts give it a homely, backyard feel. The hosts are also happy to offer guides and advice. Book well in advance. ⓐ Trakų 15–5, ⓣ 6860 4607 ⓦ www.guesthouses.info ⓝ Bus: 4, 11, 26, 43, 53; trolleybus: 1, 2, 5, 7 to Trakų

HOSTELS

A Hostel £ Not just one, but a whole cluster of new and funky hostels, one of which features Japanese-style bed pods. All locations are centred around Stepono and within easy walking distance of both the Old Town and the bus and train stations. ⓐ Sodų 17 ⓣ 5213 9994 ⓦ www.ahostel.lt

Filaretai £ The furthest away from all the Old Town action, the Filaretai is located in the alternative Užupis district (see page 82). Walking to or from this hostel is half the fun, except if you're alone and it's very late at night. It is part of the IYH network and also has bicycles available for hire. ⓐ Filaretų 17 ⓣ 5215 4627 ⓦ www.filaretaihostel.lt ⓝ Bus: 27, 34, 37, 44 to Filaretų

Old Town Hostel £ A small, comfortable, friendly and well-run hostel, conveniently located within easy walking distance of the bus and train stations. Free Wi-Fi. ⓐ Aušros Vartų 20–15 ⓣ 5262 5357

THE BEST OF VILNIUS

Getting the most out of Vilnius requires an open mind, a desire to explore, a pair of feet and the willingness to use them. Often the best things are somewhat hidden in a tucked-away courtyard or behind a door that may not look too inviting. Do be inquisitive, and don't be shy.

TOP 10 ATTRACTIONS

- **St Anne's Church** The architectural gem of Vilnius (see page 67)

- **Cathedral** Book a tour of the cellars to really delve into the city's history (see page 62)

- **KGB Museum (Museum of Genocide Victims)** Stoic, disconcerting and even a bit sickening – but a mind-opening experience (see page 66)

- **Gedimino Pilis (Higher Castle Museum)** Catch the magnificent view from the top (see page 70)

- **Applied Art Museum** Nearly all of Vilnius's arty treasures are tucked away in here (see page 69)

- **The Old Town** Charming streets, quirky courtyards, inviting cafés, and a myriad of ways to get lost (see page 62)

- **Dinner in a cellar** Burrow into Lokys (see page 75) or Žemaičiai (see page 76) for traditional *cepelinai* (see page 28) in a cellar

- **Markets** A trip to a market can be like a jaunt in a time machine – and they'll try to sell you anything (see pages 24 & 98)

- **Užupis** A trendy and alternative area, a self-designated breakaway independent republic. Look for the constitution on the wall along Paupio Gatvė (see page 85)

- **Gates of Dawn** The original 16th-century gates to the city, shielding a glowing image of the Virgin Mary (see page 64)

🔽 *Renaissance façade in the Old Town*

Suggested Itineraries

HALF-DAY: VILNIUS IN A HURRY

When you're pushed for time, concentrate on the area around the cathedral (see page 62). Here you can visit Gedimino Pilis (Higher Castle, see page 70), the Applied Art Museum (see page 69), and of course the cathedral itself. Finish off by wandering down Pilies Street to the Town Hall and back, and stop off for a quick lunch or coffee at any of the many street-side cafés.

1 DAY: TIME TO SEE A LITTLE MORE

With a little more time, you can explore the Old Town (see page 62) more fully – and that simply means walking. Head in pretty much any direction from the Town Hall and you'll find yourself in a network of charming streets. The mixture of charming and crumbling delights you will come across is fascinating. For Jewish history and culture, head south towards Geto Aukų Aikštė (Ghetto Square) and keep your eyes peeled for plaques with Yiddish inscriptions along the way.

2–3 DAYS: TIME TO SEE MUCH MORE

Squeezing in a trip to Trakai (see page 102) is a must. The town is home to a medieval-looking castle nestled on an island in a lake, with attractive greenery on all the surrounding banks.

LONGER: ENJOYING VILNIUS TO THE FULL

In summer, exploring Lithuania's fantastic national parks and lakes is sublime. If you can, take a trip to the unique UNESCO World Heritage Site of the Curonian Spit (see page 124). The Hill of Crosses in Šiauliai (see page 125) should be on your list too. Both are a fair distance from Vilnius and really deserve an overnight stay to

🔺 *Higher Castle is an icon of Vilnius*

do them justice. Closer by are Kernavė (see page 12) and Molėtai, the former boasting some interesting history and the latter an area of gorgeous lakes.

If you still have a day to spare after this, jump on a bus to Gruto Parkas near Druskininkai, a theme park filled with Lithuania's old Soviet statues of Lenin and Stalin (see page 114).

Something for nothing

The best way to enjoy Vilnius without spending a cent – or a *centas* in the local language – is to walk. Exploring the Old Town is a rewarding experience, especially if you deviate from the obvious routes and burrow into little side streets and courtyards. Slip through what may look like a private doorway, and you can discover a whole new side of the city, where one courtyard adjoins another, and then another, before leading to yet another street.

On Vokiečių Street next door to the Žemaičiai restaurant, for example, is a little doorway leading to a courtyard that, with parked cars and the back doors of restaurants, is hardly much of a discovery. At the back of this, however, is a little tunnel – you'll have to crouch to get through it – leading to another courtyard that is well worth discovering. It's a pleasant snapshot of a different way of life. Wooden balconies overlook the yard where locals sometimes sit and chat. A row of wooden storage sheds lines the other side. You've probably only walked 50 m (164 ft), but you'll feel a million miles away from the hustle and bustle of Vokiečių Street.

Another courtyard, on Rūdninkų Street near the corner of Pylimo, boasts an almost intact portion of the otherwise long-gone original city wall.

The routes through these courtyards are not marked on any map as they are actually private property. Keep this in mind as you explore; keep quiet and don't invade the residents' privacy by looking through their windows, and nobody will mind.

Large open public spaces are also worth hanging around in, especially Cathedral Square, Gedimino Prospektas and Rotušės (Town Hall) Square. On public holidays and celebrations there are often markets and fairs where you can try traditional foods as well as see locals dressed in costumes and dancing. Cathedral Square hosts regular free concerts and celebrations on holidays – ask at the tourist office if there is anything going on.

If you're in Vilnius on April Fools' Day, you'd be a fool not to head to Užupis (see page 82), the self-declared independent republic breakaway district. They'll be happy to stamp your passport and toss you into the midst of all sorts of wacky revelry on that day.

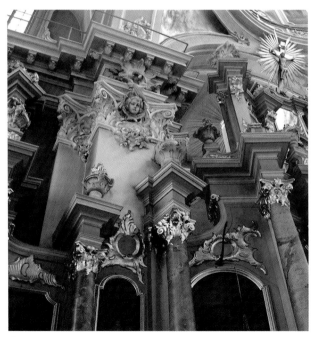

⬤ *Admire the ornate interiors of the Orthodox churches*

When it rains

There's a whole other side of Vilnius to explore when the skies open up – the city's underside. Vilnius is riddled with cellars and crypts. Most have been turned into cafés, bars and nightclubs that play on the cave-like appeal of their location. Others are museums, and others are just plain creepy. Burrowing into such places is an excellent option in bad weather.

The most obvious underground attraction is the network of crypts and rooms beneath the main cathedral (see page 62). Reasonably priced tours covering architectural, artistic and political history can be organised at the small shop located in the side of the cathedral. If you have trouble with the language, ask at the tourist office. Regular tours leave at specified times, or if there are several of you, consider hiring a private guide for your group.

Another good-value underground attraction is the Artillery Bastion, a horseshoe-shaped tunnel in the side of a hill (thankfully, it's brick entrance is easy to spot). Originally built for defensive purposes (it was once a part of the original city wall), you'll see that it has also been used to store vegetables, rubbish and, somewhat disturbingly, orphaned children.

If you prefer your history above ground, try the varied and rewarding Higher Castle Museum (see page 70). Old coins, pieces of uniform from Napoleon's troops and a wide variety of other artefacts have been dug up and presented here, along with informative descriptions in English.

● *Explore the Artillery Bastion*

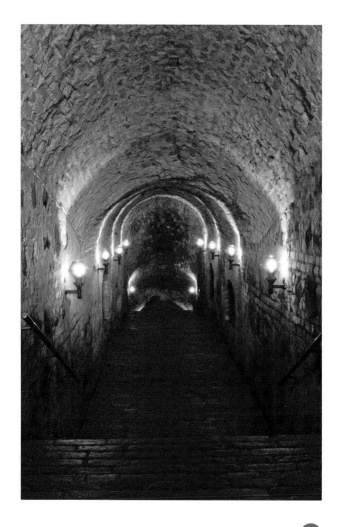

On arrival

TIME DIFFERENCE
Lithuania is two hours ahead of Greenwich Mean Time. Clocks go forward one hour in March for daylight saving and are turned back again in October.

ARRIVING
By air
Even with a new terminal just opened and renovations still underway, **Vilnius Airport** (❶ 5230 6666 Ⓦ www.vilnius-airport.lt) is a small and uncomplicated facility. It has a bureau de change and ATM machine, car-rental desks, a restaurant and café and a useful kiosk selling phonecards and tickets for public transport.

The Old Town is just 8 km (5 miles) away from the airport and should take 15 minutes in a taxi. Official rates per kilometre are written on a sign near the taxi rank outside and you should always agree on a price before setting off. The standard price is around 40–50Lt but many drivers may try to charge you more, particularly if it is late or at the weekend.

A cheaper alternative is to take bus 1 or 2 from the stop just to the left of the arrivals hall. Between three and fives buses leave every hour between 05.04 and 23.52 on weekdays and between 06.08 and 23.11 at weekends. Tickets can be bought from the driver.

Ryanair flights arrive at **Kaunas Airport** (❶ 3739 9307 Ⓦ www.kaunasair.lt), around one and a half hours from Vilnius by road. Private minibuses to the centre, timed to coincide with flight arrivals, cost 45Lt or 35Lt if you book in advance on-line (❶ 6724 5400 Ⓦ www.airport-bus.lt ❷ info@airport-bus.lt).

🔵 *The airport building is mostly in keeping with the architectural style*

You may also like to stop for a while in Kaunas – Lithuania's second largest city – before you head on to Vilnius. Bus 29 goes from the airport to Kaunas main bus and train stations, from where there are regular connections to Vilnius. On weekdays

there are two buses an hour between 05.16 and 22.25. At weekends, buses are less frequent than once an hour and run between 06.45 and 20.09.

By rail

Vilnius railway station (ⓐ Geležinkelio 16 ⓣ 5233 0088) is located within walking distance of the Old Town. If you are arriving on an international train, you will have to pass through customs. There is a small kiosk at the station, as well as ATMs and a bureau de change. See ⓦ www.litrail.lt for timetable information.

Opposite the railway station exit is McDonald's – walk past this and carry on down the gentle slope until you come to a four-way intersection with a rail bridge to the right. Turn left here and walk straight ahead. You'll soon pass through the Gates of Dawn into the Old Town.

If you don't want to walk, take bus 26, trolleybus 1, 2, 5 or 7 or minibuses 1, 2, 4, 5, 7 or 62 straight to the city centre. Taxis are plentiful and should cost around 10Lt to a central hotel.

By road

The main bus station is fairly near the railway station – walk through the station building and once outside, veer to the right. See above for directions on getting to the Old Town from here.

Inside the building you will find facilities for left luggage, offices for international bus companies including Eurolines, kiosks, cafés and ATMs.

FINDING YOUR FEET

Vilnius is a relatively small and calm city, although there is always plenty going on – especially in summer. It's the ideal city

IF YOU GET LOST, TRY ...

Excuse me, do you speak English?
Atsiprašau, Jūs kalbate angliškai?
Aht-see-prah-show, Yoos kahl-bah-teh ahng-leesh-kay?

Excuse me, is this the right way to ... the cathedral/the tourist office/the castle/the old town?
Atsiprašau, ar aš teisingai einu į ... katedrą/turistų biurą/pilį/senamiestį?
Aht-see-prah-show, ur ash tey-sing-ay ay-noo ee ... cutt-ed-rah/too-riss-too byoo-rah/peeli/seh-nah-myes-tee?

Can you point to it on my map?
Ar galite parodyti Žemėlapyje?
Ur gull-it-teh purr-oddity zhe-mell-uppie-ya?

for strolling, but be careful on narrow streets where pedestrians often spill onto the road, and the road seems to be used as a racetrack by cars, taxis and motorbikes.

It is generally a very safe place to visit, but take common-sense precautions by keeping valuables locked in your hotel safe and by not antagonising locals, especially at night.

Beggars can be a problem as they tend to be persistent. The tourist office has advised visitors not to offer money as there are soup kitchens and charitable organisations in the city which provide beggars with more reliable support. Be firm, refuse loudly and then, if they persist, simply ignore them.

ORIENTATION

Vilnius sprawls out from around the cathedral – a place where two rivers once met in a gentle valley. The smaller river Vilnia once flowed along what is now the road leading from the cathedral, Šventaragio. The area of the cathedral is a good orientation point. If you're lost, just say the word 'cathedral' to a passer-by to be pointed in the right direction.

The main attractions lie in an area the shape of a generous pie-wedge, with the cathedral at the point. One edge is the rough line between Pilies, Didžioji and Aušros Vartų streets and the area immediately east of this. The other edge runs along Gedimino Prospektas.

⬥ An easy way to get around

The streets of Vilnius, with the exception of the long and straight Gedimino Prospektas, are confusingly higgledy-piggledy. If your sense of direction is even slightly less than high-grade military GPS standard, don't go too far without a map until you get to know at least the main streets.

GETTING AROUND

Vilnius is small and compact and the best way to get around is by foot. For the few instances when something is too far away to stroll to, Vilnius's comprehensive network of trolleybuses, microbuses and ordinary buses will get you there quickly and cheaply. For comfort's sake, avoid rush hour.

Electric trolleybuses have antennae attached to cables above the road. They are most useful for the inner city centre and their routes and route numbers are marked in red on the city's transport map. Regular diesel buses tend to travel a little further into the outskirts and their routes are marked in blue. Be aware that a trolleybus and regular bus can have the same number but go to completely different destinations. The transport map on page 56 of this guide shows only trolleybuses.

The same tickets can be used for both trolleybuses and regular buses and can be purchased from kiosks marked 'Lietuvos Spauda' or from the driver for a slightly higher rate. Each ticket is valid for a single journey on a single vehicle, and must be validated in either the electronic or the older red 'crimping' devices on board.

Microbuses are licensed, commercially run, and terribly convenient. They are minibuses that tear along numbered routes, picking up and dropping off passengers as required along the way. When you see one coming, put your hand in the air to hail it. The standard rate is 3Lt for a journey, paid to the driver when you get in. Look out for your destination and as you approach make it clear that you want to get off.

Taxis are an inexact science in Vilnius and drivers can be unhelpful, sometimes charging over the odds or refusing to use their meter. A trip within the Old Town in normal hours shouldn't cost more than 20Lt. Booking a taxi in advance is actually cheaper than hailing one in the street. Some taxi firms are:

Martonas (❶ 5240 0004), **Vilniaus Taksi** (❶ 5261 6161), **Ekipažas** (❶ 5239 5539) and **Kabrioletas** (❶ 5213 2332).

CAR HIRE

The bus network and your own feet will work well enough for exploring the centre of Vilnius, but hiring a car will give you more freedom if you're planning to travel elsewhere. Navigating is easy as there are excellent road signs, but beware some rather haphazard driving from locals in the city centre. When you're on the open road, keep an eye out to avoid horses and carts or slow-moving agricultural machinery.

Most international car-rental companies operate in Lithuania but local options can be cheaper.

A&A Litinterp ⓐ Bernardinų 7–2 ❶ 5212 3850 ⓦ www.litinterp.lt

Avis ⓐ Rodūnios Kelias 2 (Airport) ❶ 5232 9316 ⓦ www.avis.lt

Budget ⓐ Rodūnios Kelias 2 (Airport) ❶ 5230 6708 (24hrs) ⓦ www.budget.lt

Europcar ⓐ Stuokos-Gucevičiaus 9–1 ❶ 5212 0207 ⓦ www.europcar.lt

Hertz ⓐ Kalvarijų 14 ❶ 5272 6940 ⓦ www.hertz.lt

Rimas Rentacar ❶ 5277 6213 ⓔ rimas.cars@is.lt

Sixt ⓐ Rodūnios Kelias 2 (Airport) ❶ 5239 5636 ⓦ www.sixt.lt

❍ *One of the many Orthodox churches in Vilnius*

Old Town

It won't take you long to see why UNESCO has listed Vilnius Old Town as a World Heritage Site. While that credential doesn't make it unique, the range of architecture on display in Vilnius does. Vilnius has a few hidden architectural treasures that easily rank as the best of their kind in Europe and possibly the world.

Much of Vilnius was shaped by the fact that many different religions and cultures were welcomed here. It was a city of tolerance and acceptance, and the wide range of immigrants all made their particular mark. At the same time, Lithuanians also eloquently expressed their culture in the built environment and the results of this combination are what you see today.

The Old Town is compact enough to get around on foot and this is by far the simplest way to navigate. If you do need to use public transport, obtain a detailed transport map from the tourist information centre and check with locals and drivers exactly which buses are going to your destination.

SIGHTS & ATTRACTIONS

Cathedral

The first cathedral on this site was erected in 1251, funded by Grand Duke Mindaugas. There were pagan temples here prior to that, evidence of which is still visible if you take a tour of the cellars (see page 48).

The current building was designed and built by Stuoka-Gucevičius between 1769–1820. The same architect was also responsible for parts of the Presidential Palace and you can see a statue of his stylised head in the little park at the end of the street which bears his name.

Old Town

0	200 metres
0	200 yards

POI
† Cathedral
i Information
✈ Airport
🚉 Railway Stn
🚌 Bus Station
✚ Hospital

THREE-HANDED SAINT

Look closely at the image of St Casimir in his chapel in the cathedral and you'll see that, apparently, he had three hands. Legend has it that the artist who created the picture decided to change the position of the hand, so he painted over it and drew a new one. The old hand, however, kept reappearing each time it was painted over. The painter eventually concluded that it must be a miracle and left the picture tri-handed.

The cathedral is home to a range of stunning chapels including, in the northeast corner, that of Lithuania's patron saint Casimir.
ⓐ Katedros Square 🕒 08.00–19.00

Gates of Dawn

The Gates of Dawn were the original 16th-century gateway to the city. Visitors had to pay to enter with a rock or stone, thereby contributing directly to the paved streets of the walled city. A chapel was built into the structure above the arched entranceway in 1671 and became home to a glowing image of the Virgin Mary. It is visible through an open window and is believed to have miraculous powers, which is why older locals, mostly ladies, still kneel in the street before it.

To really appreciate this cornerstone of Vilnius, duck into a little doorway on your left as you are facing the Virgin Mary, climb the stairs and marvel at the neoclassical interior that was decorated in 1829. Services are held here several times a day in Lithuanian only.
ⓐ Aušros Vartų 12 📞 5212 3513 🕒 07.30–18.30

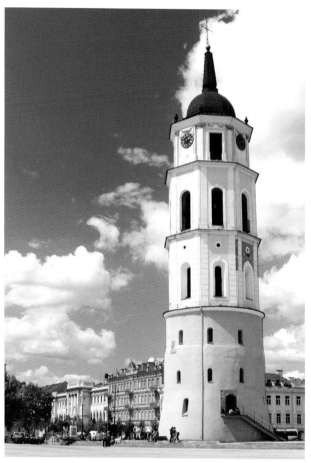

⬥ The cathedral's bell tower is a striking landmark

KGB Museum (Museum of Genocide Victims)

The former KGB and Gestapo headquarters and prison – a site of countless atrocities – now houses a stoic but chilling museum. There's no attempt to glorify or dress up the past, and there doesn't need to be. Descriptions on the walls simply state what each room was used for. The water torture room and padded cell are particularly quietening, but the execution chamber takes things to another level.

Entirely run by volunteers, the impressive no-nonsense set-up of the museum creates a completely appropriate and respectable representation of the grisly, painfully recent past. Outside the buildings, names of victims are engraved on the stones in the walls. At weekends, veterans can sometimes be seen gazing mournfully at the names and dates.

The KGB museum is not the most pleasant sight you will see on your visit, but equally it is not to be missed. Note that while the museum is officially called the Museum of Genocide Victims

SEREIKIŠKIŲ PARK

A walk along the river through this central park is a real pleasure that can easily be fitted into a busy day. Find a spot on the bank under the shade of a tree and listen to the music of the river flowing by. If you're entering the park from Cathedral Square, pick up an ice cream from the stand as you walk in.

In the daytime, you'll often see couples and young families strolling through the grounds, or students sitting reading books. By early evening, however, a different crowd arrives and you'll notice that black leather, chains and large safety pins are still popular among some young people here.

(*Genocido Aukų Muziejus*), many believe this is an inappropriate name and it is generally referred to as the KGB Museum. ❷ Aukų 2a ❶ 5249 6264 Ⓦ www.genocid.lt/muziejus ❸ 10.00–17.00 Tues–Sat, 10.00–15.00 Sun, closed Mon. Admission charge

St Anne's Church & Bernardine Church

These two churches hug the same site. The attractive one closest to the street is St Anne's, an exquisite Gothic building that, allegedly, Napoleon wanted to hold in his hand and carry back to Paris. Thirty-three different kinds of decorative bricks were used in the construction,

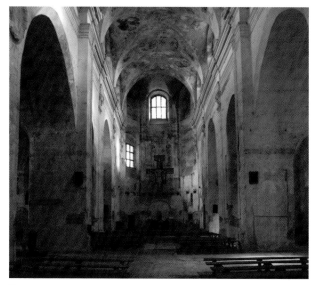

● *Interior of the Bernardine Church*

a unique method of building such a grand church and one which gives it a charming hand-made appearance.

Next door is the Bernardine Church, fairly ordinary on the outside but hiding some real treasures inside. The best entrance is actually to the right of the main door by the bottom of the ramp. As your eyes grow accustomed to the dim light, look over to the left-hand wall and you'll see some frescoes which are unique in their combination of theme and style. The first and most impressive depicts St Christopher carrying a young Jesus across a river. Further into the church, along the same wall, you will notice some partially revealed confessionals.

The courtyard between the churches is lovely and a good place for romantic or family holiday snaps. If you see a 'no photography' sign on the gate this is usually because a private formal event, such as a wedding, has just taken place. If you see the sign, just pop inside and ask at the souvenir stall if you may take photos.

ⓐ Maironio 8

CULTURE

Amber Museum-Gallery

Amber is the jewel of the Baltics – except when it contains a prehistoric insect, when it becomes compellingly curious and creepy. The Amber Museum-Gallery is really just a well-stocked shop with an excellent display downstairs showing off the main amber discoveries, different types of amber, and some inconceivably old preserved insects. Some could be 100 million years old, but their wings still look crisp in the hardened amber.

Also of note is an imitation display of the Juodkrantė Hoard, a famous collection of amber dredged up from the bottom of the

● *The Amber Museum-Gallery features some excellent displays*

Curonian Lagoon by a mining company. Despite the fact that it contains evidence of the lifestyle of Stone Age Baltic tribes the collection was quickly broken up and widely dispersed. This is one of the best amber museums in Lithuania, second only to the **Palanga Amber Museum** (Ⓦ www.pgm.lt) in the coastal town of Palanga. ⓐ Šv. Mykolo 8 ⓘ 5262 3092 ⓘ 10.00–19.00. Admission charge

Applied Art Museum

While Vilnius's Royal Palace is being reconstructed behind the cathedral, remnants of the original can be found here. What may at first look like a collection of rubble takes on new meaning when you discover something of its context, and then glance at the rapidly growing reconstruction site. There's also a fragment of the former city wall still visible in the basement.

The museum has an additional collection of art, mostly religious, dating from the 16th century. ⓐ Arsenalo 3a ⓣ 5262 8080 ⓒ 11.00–18.00 Tues–Sat, 11.00–16.00 Sun, closed Mon. Admission charge

Gedimino Pilis (Higher Castle Museum)

The highlight – literally – of this museum is its tower, all that is left of the former castle and as iconic of Vilnius as anything in the city. A climb to the top will reward you with a terrific view over Vilnius's haphazard jumble of roofs. It's worth doing this towards the beginning of your stay in order to get your bearings. Bring your camera and binoculars if you have them.

The museum itself contains a collection of medieval decoration and artefacts. One of the most interesting displays is the model of how the whole castle complex originally looked. ⓐ Castle Hill, Arsenalo 5 ⓣ 5261 7453 ⓒ 10.00–17.00 Tues–Sun, closed Mon. Admission charge

Kazys Varnelis Museum

The Lithuanian artist Kazys Varnelis spent a large amount of time in the US after escaping Soviet occupation in 1949. He focused on creating pattern-based optical illusion images on a large scale. He also collected a magnificent hoard of art and furniture covering a broad range of periods, cultures and styles.

When Varnelis returned to Lithuania in 1998 he brought his collection with him and arranged it carefully in this 33-room museum, in the order in which it remains to this day. Advance reservation

---

▶ *Take a stroll through the town*

is required to visit the museum. ❸ Didžioji 26 ❶ 5279 1644
❷ kvmuziejus@lnm.lt ❸ 10.00–17.00 Tues–Sat, closed Sun & Mon

RETAIL THERAPY

Pilies Street is the place to find souvenirs, with shops ranging from
ramshackle street-side affairs to clean, efficient stores with English-
speaking staff. You will find plentiful amber and linen products as well
as other tourist take-homes including t-shirts, flags and fridge magnets.

At the point where Pilies Street becomes Didžioji Street, there
is a small market of stalls selling local artwork as well as more
souvenirs. There are plans to move sellers to an area of wooden
market stalls just east of the Old Town, on the intersection of
Maironio and Aukštaičių Streets.

TAKING A BREAK

Balti Drambliai £ ❶ Café with a pleasant courtyard in summer.
In winter, you'll have to burrow into the basement. ❸ Vilniaus 41
❶ 5262 0875 ❸ 11.00–00.00 Mon–Fri, 12.00–00.00 Sat & Sun

Čili Kava £ ❷ Cheap and cheerful, with service at the counter.
❸ Pilies 16 ❶ 5260 9028 ❸ 07.30–22.00 Mon–Thur, 07.30–23.00 Fri,
09.00–23.00 Sat, 09.00–22.00 Sun

Coffee Inn £ ❸ Part of a chain of sandwich shops, serving good
coffee but rather pricey sandwiches and wraps. Ideal for a quick
break, especially if you prefer to see what your food looks like before
making a selection. ❸ Pilies 10 ❶ 6557 7764 ❸ 07.00–21.00 Mon-Fri,
09.00–21.00 Sat & Sun

Mano Kavinė £ ❹ A hidden favourite for locals who like the laid-back atmosphere, cheap eats, aquarium and free use of the internet. The café springs to life in the evenings. ⓐ Bokšto 7 ❶ 5215 3000 ⓦ www.manokavine.lt ❶ 11.00–02.00 Mon–Thur, 11.00–04.00 Fri & Sat, closed Sun

Pilies Kepyklėlė £ ❺ A charming café littered with doilies and cream cakes in an excellent location. The salads, crêpes and pasta dishes are delicious. Try their speciality *medaus tortas* (layered honey cake) or the biscuity, fudge-filled *tinginys* ('lazybones' cake). Free Wi-Fi. ⓐ Pilies 19 ❶ 5260 8992 ❶ 09.00–23.00

Pizza Jazz £ ❻ One of the best outlets of this chain of classy pizza joints, where you can sip white wine or a cool beer while watching people stroll past the window. ⓐ Gedimino 20 ❶ 5212 0839 ⓦ www.pizzajazz.lt ❶ 10.00–23.00 Sun–Wed, 10.00–00.00 Thur–Sat

Double Coffee £–££ ❼ Baltic-wide chain serving extremely good tea and coffee and a good range of salads, light meals, sweets and snacks. Rather pricey, but worth it for the choice and 24-hour opening. There are several locations in the Old Town, but these are the best for people-watching if you can get a street-side table. ⓐ Pilies 34 ❶ 6523 7634 ⓐ Gedimino 26 ❶ 5261 4175 ⓐ Gedimino 5 ❶ 5261 4723 ⓦ www.doublecoffee.lt ❶ Open 24 hrs

Blusyne ££ ❽ Tiny, quirky café, bar and restaurant in one, named after the owner's friendly dog. Ideal for coffee at any time but best in the evening for a meal or a glass of wine. There's outdoor seating in a secret little courtyard at the back in summer. ⓐ Savičiaus 5 ❶ 5212 2012 ⓦ www.blusyne.lt ❶ 12.00–00.00

AFTER DARK

RESTAURANTS

Bistro 18 ££ ❾ Foreign run and with friendly staff, this is a favourite of trendy types who still like the comfort of home. Simple and stylish with a crisp but cosy atmosphere, the food is a mix of modern cuisine and home-style cooking. The little wine shop to one side has a great selection. ⓐ Stiklių 18 ❶ 6777 2091 🕓 12.00–00.00 Mon–Sat, 12.00–17.00 Sun

Čingino ££ ❿ Drop in here for a Russian-style evening of food, vodka, music and loud laughter. It's a stylish brick-vaulted cellar with a tiled floor and can become very noisy when full. Food is both flavoursome and filling. You might be tempted to splash out on Russian vodka while you're here, but it's not necessary as Lithuanian vodka is much cheaper and generally just as good. ⓐ Basanavičiaus 11 ❶ 5261 5555 🕓 12.00–00.00

Dubliner ££ ⓫ Allegedly an Irish pub although run by two British owners, this is actually a proper sit-down restaurant with pleasant meals and excellent service. The prices are rather high by local standards. ⓐ Dominikonų 6 ❶ 5262 0239 🕓 11.00–00.00 Sun–Thur, 11.00–02.00 Fri & Sat

Saint Germain ££ ⓬ This long-standing restaurant's country cottage charm makes it a favourite with loyal locals. The food is modest but creative in its garnishes and sauces. Ideal for romantic dinners, family meals or a special occasion. Advance booking is advisable. ⓐ Literatų 9 ❶ 5262 1210 ⓦ www.vynine.lt 🕓 11.00–00.00

Sue's Indian Raja ££ ⑬ This authentic Indian restaurant has justifiably attracted interest from international food and travel magazines. Meals are simple but beautifully prepared and consistently good. Icons in the menu indicate the degree of spiciness. The décor is a bit over the top, with gilded furniture and pictures, but you'll still be welcome in casual dress. Service is always friendly and efficient, and Raj, the owner, will often visit diners for a chat. ⓐ Odminių 3 ☎ 5266 1888 ⓦ www.suesindianrestaurants.com ⏰ 11.00–00.00

Zoe's Bar & Grill ££ ⑭ This place burst recently onto the local dining scene amid a blaze of delays, false starts and red tape but is now well into the swing of things. The food is American-style with an occasional Asian twist, the atmosphere is bright and zesty, service is bubbly and you're guaranteed a good feed and a fun night out. ⓐ Odminių 3 ☎ 5212 3331 ⏰ 11.30–01.00 Mon–Fri, 12.00–01.00 Sat–Sun

Helios ££–£££ ⑮ The Helios centre, right next to the Town Hall, contains a nightclub, steak restaurant, Japanese restaurant, casino and sports bar. All of them are excellent, if not at all Lithuanian. The nightclub is extremely modern and popular, while the restaurants offer some of the best international food in town. ⓐ Didžioji 28 ⏰ Opening times vary according to venue

Lokys £££ ⑯ One of Vilnius's oldest, most respected restaurants, famous for offering hunters' delights such as beaver as well as traditional Lithuanian dishes. It has recently expanded to include a modern steak restaurant. Tables are in the cellars, accessed via a very narrow twisting stairway, and spread through various nooks, halls and little rooms, one of which used to be a prison cell. Wherever you choose to eat, the food is first class. On weekend evenings they often put on medieval-themed music and entertainment. Ideal for group parties. ⓐ Stiklių 8 ⓣ 5262 9046 ⓦ www.lokys.lt ⓛ 12.00–00.00

Marino £££ ⓱ Probably the most expensive fish and seafood restaurant in town but also the most outstanding. It's set dramatically in a glass tube that hangs over a road in the upmarket Vilniaus Vartai complex (see page 98). Inside, you'll find flouncy old furniture and a crayfish pond. The food and service are both excellent. ⓐ Tumėno 4 ⓣ 5240 9677 ⓦ www.marino-restaurant.lt ⓛ 11.00–23.00

Medininkai £££ ⓲ Gorgeous rooms with arched ceilings decorated with intricate frescoes give this restaurant a fairytale feeling. The food is generally very good although certainly not cheap. Service is friendly if not always efficient. The best part of the experience is the special atmosphere, which offers an evening that won't be quickly forgotten. ⓐ Aušros Vartų 6 ⓣ 5266 0771 ⓛ 12.00–00.00

Žemaičiai £££ ⓳ For an authentic adventure and some traditional food, this restaurant is hard to beat. The food is generally good and the rabbit-warren interior gives it a great atmosphere. When you enter, walk past the bar and head downstairs, taking care not to bang your head on the low ceiling. ⓐ Vokiečių 24 ⓣ 5261 6573 ⓦ www.zemaiciai.lt ⓛ 11.00–00.00

BARS & CLUBS

Briusly Pronounced 'Bruce Lee', and inspired by his films that were a black-market hit in the Soviet days, this place is frequently fizzing

with fresh-faced happy people having a good time. ⓐ Šv. Ignoto 12
ⓣ 5212 1215 ⓒ 12.00–02.00

◢ *Mixing it in one of Vilnius's many night spots*

Brodvėjus One of a few places that offer a fun and friendly atmosphere every night of the week. There's a large barn-style area downstairs with a gaggle of tables and chairs and a modest dance floor. Overlooking this is a balcony, also decked out with tables and chairs and the perfect spot for people-watching. There's a lively bar in another room downstairs, and a lounge-style room upstairs. The mix of cacophonous and crazy on the one hand and the laid-back and mellow on the other is ideal. Meals are available. 🅐 Mėsinių 4 🅣 5210 7208 🆆 www.brodvejus.lt 🅛 12.00–03.00 Sun & Mon, 12.00–04.00 Tues, 12.00–05.00 Wed–Sat

Cozy The cruisy café that sets the standard, popular with the young and trendy partly on account of the free Wi-Fi on offer. Smooth, slack style and good snacks and light meals are what it's all about. On weekend evenings, a DJ spins tunes in a cave-style lounge bar, attracting an easy-going and laid-back crowd of student types. 🅐 Dominikonų 10 🅣 5261 1137 🆆 www.cozy.lt 🅛 09.00–02.00 Mon–Wed, 09.00–04.00 Thur & Fri, 10.00–04.00 Sat, 10.00–02.00 Sun

Gras'as A curious place, decorated with grass – on the ceiling, in the toilets, and even on the lampshades. Food is decent and service is friendly and efficient. Live jazz is sometimes on and there are quieter rooms off the main area. You can also sit upstairs on a table held up by a garden gnome. 🅐 Vokiečių 2 🅣 6993 0052 🆆 www.grasas.lt 🅛 12.00–00.00 Mon–Thur, 12.00–01.00 Fri & Sat

In Vino Quintessential wine bar with a lovely local twist. Whether it be hot wine in winter, or a cool white on summer evenings in the courtyard, there's a relaxed, friendly and refined atmosphere to the place. Quickly becoming a Vilnius institution. ⓐ Aušros Vartų 7 ⓣ 5212 1210 ⓦ www.invino.lt ⓛ 16.00–02.00 Sun–Thur, 16.00–04.00 Fri & Sat

Lithuanian Wild Club Recently revamped in terms of style and service and attracting a cleaner crowd, this unpretentious but fun, safe strip club is the place to go for anything from topless dancing to a private strip show. ⓐ Gedimino 24 ⓣ 5262 4473 ⓦ www.wild.lt ⓛ 21.00–06.00 (hours vary)

Mojito Naktys This cocktail bar is as smooth as a Slippery Nipple and staffed by the sort of shakers who know the difference between a Classic Martini, a Vodka Martini and a Bradford. Frequented by a gently elite set of locals and expats, it's a groovy Vegas-style cave with an intricate cluster of little rooms scattered with padded benches and cushions. ⓐ Didžioji 33/2 (enter from Arklių street) ⓣ 6100 4131 ⓛ 19.00–02.00 Tues–Thur, 19.00–05.00 Fri & Sat, closed Sun & Mon

Pabo Latino Top Latino club with exquisite decoration, a classy clientele, and, in summer, a courtyard for outdoor dancing and lounging about under tents. Dress smartly and expect queues at the door, although Wednesday and Thursday nights are a bit more casual and cheaper. ⓐ Trakų 3/2 ⓣ 5262 1045 ⓦ www.pabolatino.lt ⓛ 20.00–01.00 Wed, 20.00–03.00 Thur, 20.00–05.00 Fri & Sat, closed Sun–Tues

Pramogų Bankas The casino's name means 'entertainment bank' and if you don't mind depositing a bit of cash you can make a whopping great withdrawal of fun. Aside from the casino, there are also a couple of bars and a swish restaurant inside. The top and bottom floors house nightclubs – head upstairs for dark lights and

lasers or downstairs for a brighter vibe and a slightly older crowd.
ⓐ Paménkalnio 7/8 ⓣ 7005 5555 ⓦ www.pramogubankas.lt
ⓛ 24 hrs; upstairs nightclub 20.00–06.00 Thur–Sat

Prospekto Pubas Dry by day, this place goes crazy at night and
becomes one of the city's hottest clubs. Watch out for cheeky
bartenders who 'assume' you want to leave tremendous tips and
have your drinks mixed with top-shelf vodka. ⓐ Gedimino 2
ⓣ 5212 0832 ⓛ 11.00–05.00

Savas Kampas Simple, relaxed bar for catching up with friends and
enjoying a drink and a snack. The two rooms at the back are dark but
pleasant, with plenty of comfortable couches. Service can be slow.
ⓐ Vokiečių 4 ⓣ 5212 3203 ⓦ www.savaskampas.lt ⓛ 08.30–00.00
Mon–Wed, 08.30–02.00 Thur, 08.30–03.00 Fri, 10.00–03.00 Sat,
10.00–00.00 Sun

Sole Luna A fresh, fun and zesty bar run by friendly Italians who know
how to fire up a good time. Popular with international students,
it has a gorgeous courtyard in summer when the action spills
out into the warm evening air. One of Vilnius's hidden treasures.
ⓐ Universiteto 4 ⓣ 5212 0925 ⓛ 17.00–04.00 Mon–Sat, closed Sun

Woo A hotspot for youngsters looking for an underground garage
feel, Woo is always swarming with groovy types on Friday and
Saturday nights. There is an interesting menu of Asian snacks
and meals. You'll have to seek it out, as it's tucked-away under
a somewhat formal-looking building. ⓐ Vilniaus 22 ⓣ 5212 7740
ⓛ 12.00–02.00 Mon–Thur, 12.00–05.00 Fri, 17.00–05.00 Sat,
closed Sun

◓ *Wandering down cobbled Pilies Street*

Užupis & Belmontas

The Užupis district is often described as having an alternative and arty aspect to it – something like Montmartre in Paris, Soho in London or Greenwich Village in New York. The reputation comes mostly from the fact that the area has half-mockingly declared itself an independent republic with its own constitution (see page 85).

The best time to visit Užupis is April Fools' Day, when the 'republic' celebrates its independence, will stamp your passport on entry, and provide all manner of entertainment for the day. At other times, the area is a charming collection of crumbling old buildings livened up by a celebrity statue of an angel. The term 'delightfully decrepit' has often been used to describe Užupis, as everything seems age-worn and weather-beaten – perfect for character-filled photographs. The Užupio Kavinė (see page 90) is the perfect place in Vilnius to have a beer by the river.

An afternoon spent in the area won't offer you much in the way of art and culture, particularly compared with the rich pickings in the Old Town, but it's a pleasant place for a quiet stroll. Visit with an open mind, and open eyes.

SIGHTS & ATTRACTIONS

Bernardinų Cemetery

Established in 1820 on a gradually eroding hill, some who were placed here for eternal rest have found the ground falling away beneath them. The cemetery contains the graves of university professors, scientists, artists and other intellectuals. You will notice that there are many Polish-sounding names on the tombstones. It's a beautiful place to visit in autumn and winter, when the

ramshackle grounds and graves clinging to the eroding hillside are sprinkled with either golden leaves or snow. ❷ Žvirgždyno 3

Hill of Three Crosses

Right near Užupis, on the same side of the river and reached via Kalnų Park is the iconic Hill of Three Crosses. Visible from most places in the Old Town, these three white crosses on top of a hill are laden with contradictory stories about their origin.

One story suggests that seven Franciscan monks were killed here by pagans, who tied them to the crosses then threw them down the hill into the river. They may in fact have been erected to commemorate Vilnius being granted the Magdeburg Rights which finally gave the town city status.

🔺 *The Three Crosses*

CONSTITUTION

As the Užupis area is something of a self-declared breakaway republic, residents have produced and ratified their own constitution. You can find the full text on a large plaque, proudly displayed on one of the walls that isn't crumbling, just a short wander down Paupio in the opposite direction to the Užupis Angel. The constitution declares, among other things, that:

People have the right to die, but it's not a duty.
People have the right to be insignificant and unknown.
A dog has the right to be a dog.
People have the right to be misunderstood.

Stalin tore the original crosses down and had them buried, but you can see some of their wreckage as you climb up to see the shiny new ones. From the top of the hill there is an excellent view over the city.

St Peter & St Paul's Church

This church is worth the trolleybus journey or twenty-minute walk out of town. The interior is home to a couple of thousand gently cavorting characters – plaster stuccoes clinging to the walls and dripping from the ceilings. It's easily one of Vilnius's hidden treasures.

The building was commissioned in 1668 and a team of Italians worked their baroque magic until the money ran out. Hence, the area around the altar is a bit plain in comparison to the rest of the interior. You'll also notice a chandelier ship floating overhead while you're in here, made from brass and a very impressive collection of clear glass marbles. It is a relatively recent addition to the church, made in Latvia in 1905. ⓐ Antakalnio 1 ⓣ 5234 0229 ⓛ 07.00–18.00 Mon–Sat, 09.00–18.00 Sun ⓝ Trolleybus: 2, 3, 4, 14, 17 heading east

Užupis Angel & Mermaid

The most prominent feature of Užupis is an angel on a stick. It's certainly one of Vilnius's most amusing and pleasing sculptures, a breath of fresh air compared to some other rather austere statues. The statue of the angel that you can now see, balancing on a golden ball and silently blowing a trumpet across the rooftops, was unveiled on 1 April 2001.

Before the angel appeared, the plinth on top of the stick was adorned with a large egg. The egg was sold at auction and now rests on another stick in the Jewish district, near the corner of Pylimo and Raugyklos Streets. It was recently decorated with floral painting, making it look rather like a large Easter egg.

The other notable statue in Užupis is the Mermaid of Užupis

GRAFFITI TRAIL

Can you find the cartoon snail? Or what about the sign that says 'sky (*dangus*) – 12 km' under an arrow that points straight up? Stencilled, hand sprayed, or simply scrawled, the smattering of graffiti on the crumbling walls of Užupis adds a certain character to the area. Whether or not you are a fan of graffiti, you'll get a deeper insight into the local mentality if you take a closer look at some of the images and phrases displayed as you wander around.

◒ *Vision of an angel*

● *The floral egg on its nest*

(*Užupio Mergelė*), set into a little cove in the wall of the river opposite the Užupio Kavinė café. One memorable winter morning she disappeared and was found some time later, carried downriver with the ice floes. It turned out that the ice forming around her bottom had squeezed her out of place and thrown her into the frozen river. She also took a dip when the river swelled during flooding in 2005.

WALKS

This area is great for peaceful strolling through streets and parks. Good walks are from the Užupis area to the Kalnų Park and the Hill of Three Crosses (see page 84), into Sereikiškių Park (see page 66), and also to St Peter and St Paul's Church (see page 85). If you fancy a longer stroll, head out to Belmontas (see page 91). Invest in a detailed map to avoid getting lost, particularly in some of the parks.

For a walk combined with a bit of culture, start from the bridge where Užupio crosses the river, walk either over or under the outdoor seating deck of Užupio Kavinė, and then follow the river. Along here are some interesting artists' workshops. Some of the artwork, mainly sculpture, can be seen placed outside along the river. The workshops here are rather bohemian and opening hours vary wildly.

CULTURE

TaDas Gallery

TaDas Gutauskas – the spelling is a deliberate gesture – is a prolific Vilnius-born artist who churns out sculptures, paintings and textiles. You can visit his gallery space and browse creations that range from simply refreshing and innocently fun to cringe-makingly kitsch. Call in advance to arrange a visit. ⓐ Užupio 3–5 ⓣ 5215 4550 ⓦ www.tadasgutauskas.lt

RETAIL THERAPY

Most of the shops in Užupis are the type that sell little other than cheese, lentils, beads and second-hand clothes. The alternative, anti-capitalist, anti-commercialism of Užupis means that gift and souvenir shops are thin on the ground, although one or two more upmarket interior decoration outlets are starting to pop up. Nothing is permanent in this area, so just take a stroll and see what you find.

TAKING A BREAK

Prie Angelo £ ❶ The cool little café right beside the angel is clean and fresh but still has an alternative feel to it. The furniture is wrought-iron artwork covered with cushions and there are a few angels stuccoed to the walls here and there. Pizzas and other more pleasing options are on the menu. ⓐ Užupio 9 ❶ 5215 3790 ⓛ 09.00–23.00 Sun–Thur, 09.00–00.00 Fri & Sat

Užupio Kavinė £ ❷ A lovely spot to sit by the river and listen to the music of the water. Popular with locals in summer. The drinks are better than the food. ⓐ Užupio 2 ❶ 5212 2138 ⓛ 10.00–23.00

AFTER DARK

Joana Carinova Tavern ££ ❸ Traditional Lithuanian meals are on offer in this impressive Belmontas restaurant bristling with stuffed animals and antlers. At weekends you can eat in a rather more civilised hall upstairs, but either way the food is excellent. ⓐ Belmonto 17 ❶ 6861 4656 ⓦ www.belmontas.lt ⓛ 12.00–23.00 Sun–Thur, 12.00–00.00 Fri & Sat

BELMONTAS

Once a water mill with a small and shady inn on the side, this area has now become a huge complex of restaurants and relaxing spots. There are three restaurants here, including Joana Carinova Tavern (see page 90) and Villa Gloria (see below), and plans for more.

Even if you don't fancy a meal, walking around the pleasant surroundings is a joy. You can explore the water mill itself as well as taking a walk through the Pavilniai Regional Park.

Belmontas is a good 40-minute walk from Užupis, most of it along the side of a narrow road. A taxi from the Old Town should cost no more than 25Lt.

Tores ££ ➍ There is only one venue of interest in Užupis after the sun goes down – Tores. Nestled on a hill overlooking the Old Town, the superb view is somewhat let down by the food and gruff service. Downstairs is a cabaret-style club with shows most nights at 22.00. ⓐ Užupio 40 ➊ 5262 9309 ⓦ www.tores.lt ➌ 11.00–00.00

Villa Gloria £££ ➎ This is the most upmàrket restaurant in the Belmontas complex and the ideal venue if you want to splash out – not least because it has a small swimming pool in the middle of the dining room. The wine list is outstanding, but so are some of the prices. ⓐ Belmonto 17 ➊ 6152 0220 ⓦ www.belmontas.lt ➌ 12.00–22.00 Sun–Thur, 12.00–23.00 Fri & Sat

Central & New Vilnius

Outside of the Old Town, Vilnius loses much of its quaint charm but none of its interest. It's an area of contrasts. You'll see everything from gleaming glass office towers to some raw, brash outcrops of the Soviet era. You can dine in exquisite and refined luxury, or see people pushing broken shopping trolleys loaded with carcasses at the market. This area, coarse and real, is where things can take on a decidedly gritty and bizarre edge.

SIGHTS & ATTRACTIONS

Church of St Michael & St Konstantine

This Orthodox church is most notable for the enormous green onions that stand out garishly against a blue sky, when there is one. What's behind the colour scheme, with its violent green roof, is a local mystery. ⓐ Basanavičiaus 27

Frank Zappa Statue

One of the more curious sculptures in Vilnius is that of the head of Frank Zappa, the deceased American musician and film director, mounted on a post. Zappa has nothing to do with Vilnius as such, but it was commissioned in 1995, two years after his death, by students in the city, who convinced authorities to allow it by arguing that Mr Zappa looked a bit Jewish. The sculpture was created by Konstantinas Bogdanas, who had previously honed his sculpting skills on the head of Lenin in Moscow. ⓐ Kalinausko 1

Television Tower & Akropolis

ŠNIPIŠKĖS

Vichy Aqua Park

Kalvaniju Market

T NARBUTO

KONSTITUCIJOS PROSP

Europa Shopping Mall

EUROPOS SQUARE

Neris

A GOŠTAUTO

UPĖS

POI
Cathedral
Information
Airport
Railway Stn
Bus Station
Hospital

ŽALIASIS TILTAS

ŽVEJŲ

LUKIŠKIŲ SKG

LUKIŠKIŲ

Vilniaus Vartai

A TUMENO

Parliament

National Library

GYNĖJŲ

KRAŽIŲ

J SAVICKO

ANASTOJI

J TUMO-VAIŽGANTO

VASARIO 16-OSIOS

ŠERMUKSNIŲ

KAŠTONŲ

A JAKŠTO

ŽYGIMANTŲ

TILTO

Opera & Ballet Theatre

VILNIAUS

A VIENUOLIO

GEDIMINO PROSPEKTAS

J JASINSKIO

A ROTUNDO

DAIMANTŲ

PAKALNĖS

GELEŽINIO VILKO

TAURO

PAMĖNKALNIO

KGB Museum

ALSNU

PAMĖNKALNIO

A STULGINSKIO

T LEVELELIO

GEDIMINO PROSPEKTAS

A SMETONOS

JOGAILOS

TINDŽIŲ

VILNIAUS

LABDARIŲ

CENTRE

V KUDIRKOS

M VALANČIAUS

MYKOLAIČIO-PUTINO

ŽEMAITĖ

ŠVIEAŲ

ISLANDIJOS

LIEJYKLOS

SV IGNOTO

KLAIPĖDOS

VILNIAUS

Vingio Park

J ŠIRAKAUSKO

Z SIERAKAUSKO

SUBAČIŲ

Frank Zappa Statue

PYLIMO

MK ČIURLIONIO

PYLIMO

J BASANAVIČIAUS

SVYRGAILOS

VYTENIO

MUTUVOS

ŠVIESOS

K KALINAUSKO

MINDAUGO

TEATRO

Church of St Michael & St Konstantine

Russian Drama Theatre

J BASANAVIČIAUS

TRAKŲ

Ensemble of Palaces

KĖDAINIŲ

PRANCŪSKŲ

S KONARSKIO

RASEINIŲ

IGNOTU

PYLIMO

A VIVULSKIO

ALGIRDO

MINDAUGO

NAUGARDUKO

T ŠEVČENKOS

VINGRIŲ

PYLIMO

ŽEMAITIJOS

VINGRIŲ

LIGONINĖS

Central & New Vilnius

0 _____ 500 metres

0 _____ 500 yards

🔺 *A tribute to the esteemed Mr Zappa*

Parliament

The Parliament buildings themselves are rather boxy and uninteresting, but head round to the west side of the building to see a monument consisting of assembled blocks of concrete. These blocks were part of a barrier that was used to defend the Parliament against Soviet tanks, which were trying to storm it in January 1991.
ⓐ Gedimino 53

Vichy Aqua Park

Polynesian-themed aqua park filled with tangled waterslides, a splashy kids' play area, a few pool bars, a wave pool, an artificial indoor beach and several saunas. You'll often see Polynesian performances taking place. It's all a bit plastic-fantastic, but certainly good fun. Surprisingly, it's especially nice in winter, when you can soak in a warm pool inside while snow piles up outside. ⓐ Ozo 14c ⓣ 5211 1112 ⓦ www.vandensparkas.lt ⓛ 12.00–22.00 Mon–Thur, 10.00–22.00 Fri–Sun. Admission charge

Žaliasis Tiltas

The first bridge to span the Neris was built here in 1536 and boasted a roof and shops. It has been damaged or destroyed and rebuilt several times, most recently in 1952. The current Green Bridge holds four statues that are the only remains of communist propaganda in Vilnius, constructed in the stern, proud style of socialist realism. *Agriculture* was sculpted by Bučas and Vaivada, *Industry* by Petrulis and Vyšniauskas, *Peace* by Pundzius and *Youth* by Mikėnas and Kėdainis. It's easy to look at them with a wry smile today and, given that they haven't been destroyed, decapitated or even defaced, one can only assume that the locals who lived under communism have learned to do just that.

CULTURE

Russian Drama Theatre

This old-style theatre offers a wide variety of theatrical performances, not just Russian drama. The seating can be awkward but it is generally quiet and has an atmosphere of easy-going culture. Students often come here, reading a book while waiting for a performance to begin, and in some ways it feels a bit more honest and genuine than a slick, modern theatre experience. ⓐ Basanavičiaus 13 ⓣ 5262 7133

TELEVISION TOWER

The Vilnius TV Tower is the tallest building in Lithuania. At 326 m (1,070 ft) with the aerial included, it is even a couple of metres taller than the Eiffel tower. The revolving café at the 165 m (540 ft) mark offers views over the city.

The main reason for visiting is historical. On 13 January 1991, the TV Tower punctured history when it became the centre of an assault by Soviet tanks. Thirteen unarmed Lithuanians were killed on that evening and many more were injured. The event provoked international outrage and condemnation and became a turning point in the collapse of the Soviet regime. There is a memorial and photographic exhibition at the base of the tower that is well worth a visit and a few moments of stoic silence. ⓐ Sausio 13-osios 10 ⓣ 5252 5333 ⓦ www.lrtc.lt ⓛ 10.00–21.00. Admission charge

RETAIL THERAPY

Akropolis A large shopping centre with a wide range of fashion and food shops as well as one of the best bookstores in all of Lithuania. One shelf is dedicated to English-language books. Akropolis is also a good entertainment centre, with cinemas and an ice-skating rink thoughtfully placed in the middle. ⓐ Ozo 25 ⓣ 5248 4848 ⓦ www.akropolis.lt ⓛ 08.00–00.00

Europa This small, modern shopping centre, occupying the lower floors of a shiny elliptical tower, offers mostly fashion stores, a few restaurants, and a supermarket. On the second floor, there are

⬤ *Vilnius TV Tower with the Liberty Statue at night*

egg-shaped pods protruding from the balcony which provide interesting seating for some of the cafés. ⓐ Konstitucijos 7a ⓘ 5248 7070 ⓛ Shops 10.00–22.00, Restaurants 08.00–00.00

Kalvarijų Market A stubbornly old-fashioned and authentic market experience in a city which is striving to become shiny and new. It's a huge outdoor expanse sprawling with stalls and swarming with bargain-hunters. Hours can be spent simply wandering around enjoying the hustle and bustle of it all, but keep in mind that some of the goods you purchase might not last that long. ⓐ Kalvarijų 61 ⓛ Early–13.00 Tues–Sun, closed Mon

Vilniaus Vartai As flash as it gets in Vilnius. This is the newest retail extravaganza, awash with opportunities for high-end shopping. Expect all the top-end brands and eye-popping, budget-busting prices. You won't find much that you can't find in other Western shopping centres, but if that's what you're looking for this is the place to go. ⓐ Tumėno 4 ⓦ www.vilniausvartai.lt

TAKING A BREAK

Vingio Park £ ❶ The enormous, untended park could occupy you for hours. In the middle is a huge arena which is often used for concerts. There's also a reasonable café-style restaurant behind the arena, with a small area for children to play in.

AFTER DARK

It's best to stay in the Old Town for dinner and head out to this area when you want to dance.

RESTAURANTS

Fortas £ ❷ Cleverly divided into different areas for different styles of dining, you can come here to sit at the bar, slump on a sofa, or eat at a table that appears to be in someone's living room. ❸ Algirdo 17 ❶ 5265 2526 ❷ 08.00– 24.00 Mon–Thur, 11.00–00.00 Sat, 12.00–00.00 Sun, closed Fri

BARS & CLUBS

Gravity Gravity was a bomb shelter in days gone by and you'll still enjoy the novelty of entering through a long concrete tunnel. It used to be an iconic club in Vilnius but its heyday is passed – or else, the world's clubbing scene has moved on in terms of décor and lighting and left this one behind. The music is still good and international DJs are often billed, so it's worth a try even if the place feels a bit stale. ❸ Jasinskio 16 ❶ 5269 1880 ❿ www.clubgravity.lt ❷ 22.00–05.00 Fri & Sat, closed Sun–Thur

● *The right bank of the River Neris at night*

Men's Factory Vilnius's only gay club, but you don't have to be gay to go there. In fact, it's increasingly popular with local girls who want to have fun without being hassled. Recently fitted out with fun phallic furniture and iron cobwebs, it would be a shame not to go there just to see it. The music tends to be of the heavy-rhythm techno kind. Note that security is very tight, with airport-style metal detectors at the entrance. Mobile phones with built-in cameras have to be handed over to the bouncers before they will let you in. **ⓐ** Ševčenkos 16 **ⓣ** 6998 5009 **ⓦ** www.gayclub.lt **ⓛ** 22.00–04.00 Wed & Thur, 22.00–07.00 Fri & Sat, closed Sun–Tues

Pacha This recently opened club is part of a well-known international nightclub chain and is expected to climb quickly up there among the best clubs in town. Nothing's predictable in Vilnius, so this all depends on their ability to throw a good party and attract a consistently good crowd. Certainly worth checking out for Pacha fans. **ⓐ** Gynėjų 14 **ⓣ** 6202 2044 **ⓦ** www.pachavilnius.lt **ⓛ** 22.00–06.00 Fri & Sat, closed Sun–Thur

Sky Bar The cocktail bar at the top of the Reval Hotel offers stunning views over the Old Town. Binoculars are available on request. The clientele are classy, so come dressed smartly to fit in. Prices are also sky high, but it's worth it for an evening. This is also one of only a few places with a dedicated smoking room, popular since smoking in all restaurants, bars and clubs was banned at the start of 2007. **ⓐ** Konstitucijos 20 (Reval Hotel Lietuva) **ⓣ** 5231 4823 **ⓦ** www.revalhotels.com **ⓛ** 16.00–01.00 Sun–Thur, 16.00–02.30 Fri & Sat

---

ⓞ *Trakai Castle*

Trakai

If you've bought any postcards or coffee-table books full of pretty pictures of Lithuania, Trakai will need no introduction. It's the image of the gorgeous castle on an island in the middle of a lovely lake, which looks like something out of a fairytale. While there is no doubt that the castle is Trakai's central attraction, there's more to the town than that and it is certainly worth a half- or full-day trip. Almost all visitors leave as the sun goes down as there are not many options for nightlife or accommodation – one of the best for both is the Apvalaus Stalo Klubas (see page 109). Avoid going to Trakai on Monday and Tuesday when the main attractions are closed.

GETTING THERE

Trakai is about 25 km (16 miles) from Vilnius, and can easily be visited in half a day. The most convenient option is to take a shuttle bus, either organised by your hotel or through a tour company.

A cheaper option is to go by regular bus. Buses to Trakai depart from Vilnius bus station roughly every hour with a journey time of around half an hour. The bus station is not near the town, so follow the road in the same direction as the bus was heading for about 20 minutes until you come across the main part of the settlement and the iconic castle.

A taxi from Vilnius to Trakai should cost around 900Lt, but it may be difficult to get a taxi back.

SIGHTS & ATTRACTIONS

Trakai Castle

Trakai Castle dates back to the 14th century but was almost completely destroyed during conflicts with the Russians during the 17th and 18th centuries. Restoration has been a stop-start affair since 1905.

Efforts made by imperial Russian authorities were interrupted by war, and the Soviet authorities subsequently decided that rebuilding the castle would be an inappropriate celebration of Lithuania's feudal past and brought the works to a halt again. Recent restoration took place in the 1980s and 1990s, giving the castle's magical, medieval appearance a fresh boost. The castle is used occasionally as a location for period drama involving kings and queens and knights in shining armour.

There is a worthwhile museum inside the castle, but just walking around the outside is also a pleasure. You can get a watery perspective by hiring a sailing boat (and someone to sail it) from the bridge leading up to the castle. ⓐ Pilies Island ⓘ 5285 3946 ⓛ 10.00–18.00 Tues–Sun, closed Mon. Admission charge

CULTURE

Karaite Ethnographic Museum

Some will say they were 'invited' while others will say they were 'enslaved', but whichever way you look at it, a group of Karaite people from the Crimea came to Trakai in the 15th century to act as bodyguards for Lithuania's Grand Duke Vytautas. If you fancy more

ⓓ *Preparing to sail past Trakai Castle*

THE KARAITE PEOPLE
A small community of the original Karaite immigrants' descendents still live in Trakai today and have maintained their customs, culture and language. You can eat their food, look at their little coloured wooden houses (each of which has only three windows – one for God, one for the family and one for the Grand Duke), and sometimes see them standing by their front gates in traditional dress selling trinkets.

than a cursory glance at this fascinating community, a visit to the Karaite Ethnographic Museum is a must. ② Karaimų 22 ❶ 5285 5286 🕐 10.00–18.00 Wed–Sun, closed Mon & Tues. Admission charge

RETAIL THERAPY

As summer arrives along with the tourists, stalls pop up around the shores of the lake selling cheap sunglasses, jewellery, hot dogs, amber, ice creams and all manner of souvenirs. Note, however, that of all those items, the hot dogs will probably prove to be the best value and most durable. It's actually a credit to the community at Trakai that no more intrusive and permanent gift-shops have blighted the pleasant little village.

TAKING A BREAK

The restaurants listed below are dotted along the shore facing the castle, but one of the best options for eating and drinking in Trakai is to take a picnic. Why not eat your lunch and sip some bubbly on

◐ *Pretty houses in a Trakai side street*

○ *Beautiful sunset over the lake in Trakai*

a gently drifting boat? Alternatively, stroll over to one of the less populated but equally pretty banks of the lake to enjoy the view in peace and quiet.

Kibininė £ While this place has a bit less to offer in terms of atmosphere, it is probably the best choice for trying *kibinai*, the traditional Karaite dish that can be found here. *Kibinai* are essentially hot, steaming pastry pockets full of spicy, juicy meat and onions. @ Karaimų 65 ✆ 5285 5865 🕓 10.00–22.00

Kybyniar £ This tastefully decorated little cottage offers a homely but not at all unsophisticated spot for lunch. It doesn't have a castle view but the cooking is above par for the area. *Kibinai* are served here also. @ Karaimų 29 ✆ 5285 5179 🕓 11.00–21.00 Mon–Thur, 12.00–21.00 Fri & Sat, closed Sun

AFTER DARK

There is not much in the way of nightlife in Trakai, apart from the occasional rave-style event in summer. Watching the sun set over the castle is awesome, as is spending a few moments looking at the castle lit up after dark, but after that there's no reason to hang around.

Apvalaus Stalo Klubas ££ The name means the 'round table club', but they could also have justifiably called it the 'best view'. The vista here is wonderful, looking out across the lake towards the castle. Bear in mind that the castle is lit in the evenings, so even an after-dark meal here is an experience.

There are actually two different restaurants in this same venue. Closest to the castle is the fine-dining restaurant, with fine linen, chairs wearing what look like dresses, and the best view of the castle to enjoy as you dine on French-style food. Nearby is a more casual pizzeria-style place offering pizzas and other dishes. Weather permitting, there are plenty of places to sit outdoors and even a pontoon for meals afloat.

Accommodation is also available here in the form of romantic rooms overlooking the castle. ⓐ Karaimų 53a ⓣ 5285 5595 ⓦ www.asklubas.lt ⓛ Restaurant 12.00–22.00, Pizzeria 11.00–22.00

Csarda ££ Recently opened, the Csarda has no view and needs seeking out, but still draws in the crowds with its good reputation and hearty, tasty Hungarian food. Hungarian wine and vodka are also on offer. If you're not hungry for Hungarian, there are also plenty of international and Lithuanian-style meals on the menu. If you're staying in Trakai for more than a day or two and have had your fill of castle views, this is well worth the short taxi ride. ⓐ Aukštadvario 28a ⓣ 6162 9011 ⓛ 12.00–23.00 Mon–Fri, 12.00–00.00 Sat, 12.00–22.00 Sun

● *Trakai Castle dates from the 14th century*

Druskininkai

This is Lithuania's spa-resort town, famed for its salty spring waters. The name Druskininkai comes from the Lithuanian word for salt (*druska*), and the whole town was formed around the salty springs. Local spas also specialise in mud, hot rocks, beating you with hot, wet branches and other earthy forms of therapy and pampering.

In just the last few years, Druskininkai has been rapidly growing in popularity and earning quite a reputation not just for the health resorts, but also for active holidays and romantic weekends. New hotels have been popping up and the standard of service and accommodation has been steadily increasing, although the homely, simple options still remain. Druskininkai successfully combines a basic and natural kind of appeal with as many, or as few, modern luxuries and conveniences as you may wish.

GETTING THERE

Druskininkai is roughly 130 km (80 miles) from Vilnius. There are several buses a day from Vilnius bus station to Druskininkai. Keep in mind that some buses headed for Warsaw will pass through Druskininkai, adding to the options. Buses to Druskininkai leave more frequently from Kaunas than from Vilnius, so if you're planning to visit Kaunas, it might be a good option to save your visit for there.

If driving, follow signs first to Kaunas, and then take the turn-off to Trakai. After that, there are signs to Druskininkai. Journey time is about two hours in a bus or an hour and a half by car.

● *Lake Druskonis is a peaceful spot*

SIGHTS & ATTRACTIONS

Architecture

Architectural contrast is a strong feature of Druskininkai and something to look out for. While parts of the town are being developed and appear shiny, new and fresh, there is still plenty of bizarre 1960s style architecture to make wandering around town a fascinating visual experience.

Health resorts in the Soviet era were all, for some reason, made to look like concrete fossils of space ships. For an excellent example, stroll around the building at Vilniaus 11, which has recently been developed into a sparkling new water park but still retains many elements of the original architecture. Contrasting again with both the new buildings and the old Soviet constructions are the scattering of little wooden buildings, often covered in flaking coloured paint.

GRUTO PARKAS (SOVIET STATUE PARK)

Nicknamed 'Stalinworld', this Soviet statue theme park is undoubtedly the single must-see attraction anywhere near Druskininkai or indeed anywhere near Vilnius. Many of Lenin's statues and a small selection of the Stalins that were scattered around Lithuania have ended up here. What is most interesting at Gruto Parkas, however, is not the towering communist statues themselves but the theme-park presentation of them, and the merrily mocking way the locals interact with the display.

In what can seem a curious turnaround, people who would once have shuffled grudgingly past these statues now turn up to pull faces at them, pose for photos, or just point and laugh.

◯ *Communist statues in Gruto Parkas tell a story*

Such behaviour is, of course, not without controversy, but it seems that many Lithuanians have concocted a recipe for dealing with a miserable past that contains more humour than aimless hatred. It's something that those who never lived under the Soviet regime can't really claim to understand. But you can watch.

The statues are arranged unprotected along a path. You can go and stand beside them, put your handbag on their heads, pretend to be wiping their noses or ramming an umbrella into their ears. Most of the statues and busts are accompanied by a small panel with a photo and description of the original location. In the case of the huge statue of Lenin that stood in Vilnius's Lukiškių Aikštė, the now-empty 'Red Square' on Gedimino, there is a dramatic photo of the statue being knocked down. You can also see one of only three statues ever made of Lenin having a well-earned sit down.

Also dotted along the path are guard towers that make a mockery of a concentration camp and speakers cranking out cheesy Soviet propaganda music. It all adds up to quite a strange experience. Be aware that much of the park is set around small lakes which attract swarms of blood-sucking mosquitoes in summer.

To get to Gruto Parkas, just mention the park to the driver of any bus that is going between Vilnius and Druskininkai and he will be happy to show you where to disembark. From the bus stop, it's about 1 km (1/2 mile) by foot down a signposted side road. ❸ Druskininkai ❶ 3135 5511 ❿ www.grutoparkas.lt ❶ 09.00–17.00. Admission charge

⬥ *The park is full of imposing statues*

⬥ A café in Druskininkai with a rustic setting

CULTURE

Forest Echo Museum

This temple to wood – itself made of the material and set among trees by the side of the road – contains countless beautiful wooden creations from all over Lithuania. You'll see bus stops shaped like mushrooms, pagan 'totem' poles, wooden crosses, children's playthings shaped like animals and more. Don't forget to make a call on the wooden telephone while you're here. ⓐ M K Ciurlionio 116 ⓣ 3135 3901 ⓦ www.dmu.lt ⓛ 10.00–18.00 Wed–Sun, closed Mon & Tues. Admission charge

TAKING A BREAK

If you're in Druskininkai, you're already taking a break. When you need to take a break from your break, however, try:

Regina £ A pleasant hotel restaurant, ideal for an evening meal with good company or a good book. ⓐ T Kosciuškos 3 ⓣ 3135 9060 ⓦ www.regina.lt ⓛ 08.00–23.00

Sicilia £ Essentially a pizza joint spread over two buildings – both places are casual and atmospheric and serve quality food. They are located near each other in a pleasant garden setting, one by a river. ⓐ Taikos 9 & Čiurlionio 56 ⓦ www.sicilia.lt ⓛ 10.00–23.00 Sun–Thur, 10.00–00.00 Fri & Sat

AFTER DARK

Dangaus Skliautas £ Druskininkai has a way of sprinkling everything with strangeness and this place is certainly no exception. It's a low-key restaurant most evenings, but can become interesting at the weekend when it transforms into a nightclub and you get tangled in the boudoir curtains that dangle about some of the dining booths. ⓐ Kurorto 8 ⓘ 3135 1819 ⓛ 11.00–00.00

Kolonada £ This music club and restaurant was first established in 1928 and still has an air of elegance and charm that seems somehow to stem from that era – although that doesn't mean you have to wear shapeless dresses or smoke with a long cigarette holder. The club was cleaned up and reopened in 2004 and has been attracting a good range of jazz, blues, rock 'n' roll and classic performances. Weekends are the best time to go. ⓐ Kudirkos 22 ⓘ 3135 1222 ⓦ www.kolonada.lt ⓛ 11.00–23.00 Mon–Fri, 10.00–01.00 Sat, 10.00–00.00 Sun

ACCOMMODATION

Regina ££ They've got the balance of uncomplicated comfort just right here – it's pleasant enough for a weekend away with someone special, while also affordable. The hotel also offers some very attractive package deals that include the use of the health resort and spa facilities. ⓐ T Kosciuškos 3 ⓘ 3135 9060 ⓦ www.regina.lt

Spa Vilnius ££ From the outside, this health spa looks like something that just fell to earth from space. It's the place to come for a 'trip' into health land, where they cannot only put you up for the night, but also smother you in mud, massage you with rocks, and so on. ⓐ Dineikos 1 ⓘ 3135 9160 ⓦ www.spa-vilnius.lt

Europa Royale ££–£££ A renovated 18th-century manor is now home to one of the most swish hotels in town, with rooms that come complete with an abundance of luxury. ⓐ Vilniaus 7 ⓣ 3134 2221 ⓦ www.europaroyale.com

🔺 *Druskininkai's Russian Orthodox church*

Klaipėda

Lithuania's coastal region centres around the seaport of Klaipėda, the former Prussian city of Memel. It's a long way from Vilnius — 300 km (186 miles) as the crow flies and nearly four hours on a bus or five on the train — but worthwhile if you are spending any more than a short time in Lithuania. It's particularly attractive in summer.

From Klaipėda you can easily visit either the Curonian Spit or Palanga. The Curonian Spit (see page 124) is a long finger of land that pokes out from Kaliningrad into the Baltic Sea and comes close to touching Klaipėda at its tip. The top half of the spit is Lithuanian territory, while the bottom half is Russian. The entire Curonian Spit is an area of unique and beautiful nature, and tends to be very tranquil even in summer. Palanga is a crowded, raucous beach-and-party town in summer and a popular destination for those looking for easy fun. In off-peak seasons, it is a pleasant and quiet village in a lovely seaside location.

GETTING THERE

Buses leave from Vilnius bus station to Klaipėda at 06.00, 06.35, 07.00 (summer only), 07.20, 08.50, 11.35 and 14.50. Other, slower, buses wiggle their way through a string of small villages on the way, but that drags the journey time out to something like six hours.

Trains can also whisk you across Lithuania to Klaipėda. You can check the latest schedules on the website of **Lithuanian Railways** (Ⓦ www.litrail.lt). Avoid the English-language version as this does

---

Ⓓ *A constant military presence in Klaipėda*

not list all trains. On the Lithuanian version, simply choose the 'from' (*iš*) and 'to' (*i*) stations from the drop-down menu.

SIGHTS & ATTRACTIONS

Cat and Mouse

Tucked away in the heart of the Old Town are two little statues that are sure to raise a smile. The exact locations are kept secret as stumbling across them or trying to find them is half the fun. The cat sculpture (by the sculptor Midvikis) appears to have prosthetic limbs and a splendid moustache, and the mouse (by Plotnikovas and Jurkus) proudly displays radar-dish ears. The mouse will, allegedly, listen to your wishes if you whisper into its ears.

The Curonian Spit

Many of the best attractions and distractions around Klaipėda are not in the town itself but on the Curonian Spit. A passenger ferry (ⓐ Zvejų 8 ⓣ 4631 1117 ⓦ www.keltas.lt) shuffles to and from the town and the spit on a pretty much non-stop basis, although you should check the last return time before you set out to make sure you don't end up stranded. You should not count on getting back much later than 23.00 in summer.

The return ferry ride from Klaipėda to the Curonian Spit costs around 2Lt. Bikes are charged at 2Lt extra. When the ferry docks at Smiltynė, there will be various buses and taxis offering to take you down the spit to Juodkrantė and Nida (see page 125), the two main destinations along the way.

To get across in a car, follow the signs to the more southern car-only ferry terminal, about a five-minute drive out of town at

HILL OF CROSSES

One advantage of travelling to Klaipėda on the earlier train is that it will stop in Šiauliai at about 09.20. This is home to the famed Hill of Crosses and you can easily get off the train in Šiauliai, visit the hill, spend some time exploring Šiauliai itself, and then continue on to Klaipėda. Trains from Šiauliai to Klaipėda conveniently leave at 17.10 (arriving at 20.08) and 19.40 (arriving at 21.44).

The **Šiauliai tourist information office** (❶ 4152 3110 ⓦ www.siauliai.lt/tic) will also be able to help in planning a visit, including making arrangements for a taxi to the Hill of Crosses.

Nemuno 8. The basic fare for a car and driver is 40Lt with extra charged for each passenger.

Klaipėda Hotel

The huge Klaipėda Hotel building was built in two halves forming a 'K' shape. Zip up to the 21st floor for spectacular views of the city and the tip of the Curonian Spit. There's a café and restaurant at the top but the food is rather overpriced – it's best to feed your hungry eyes on the surrounding landscape instead. ⓐ Naujojo Sodo 1 ❶ 4622 8800 ⓦ www.klaipedahotel.lt ⓛ 12.00–03.00

Nida Dunes

If it were not covered in all those hand-planted pine trees, the whole Curonian Spit (see page 124) would just blow away. As such, there are not many parts of the spit that are not wooded, but you can still see the beautiful naked dunes just south of Nida. It's well worth exploring the area as it gives you not just stunning views but a good sense of just how fragile the whole area is.

Stick to the numerous paths – if you follow them in a general upwards direction you'll come across an old sundial. This broken obelisk, sticking out of an arrangement of various tiles, was smashed to pieces by a hurricane some time ago. You can still see, however, the engravings of ancient-looking runes around the dial.

Looking south from the sundial you are actually looking into Russia. If you've got good eyes, a good zoom lens or binoculars, you will be able to make out a line of black flags sticking out of the dunes marking the border.

Sea Museum

A short walk to the right from the passenger ferry will take you to the Sea Museum, which consists of some outdoor attractions (old boats, old shacks) and the big crowd pleaser – the aquarium. Housed in a rather curious building that was once a fort, you will find all manner of fishy things to feast your eyes on, including sharks, ravenous piranha, electric eels and invisible deadly jellyfish. The interior of the building itself is also fun and the kids will love the performing dolphins and sea lions. ⓐ Smiltyne 3 ⓣ 4649 0740 ⓛ 10.30–18.30 Tues–Sun, June–Aug; 10.30–18.00 Wed–Sun, May & Sept; 10.30–17.00 Sat & Sun, Oct–April. Admission charge

Simon Dach Fountain

The German poet Simon Dach (1605–51) is commemorated by a fountain that contains a statue of Aennchen von Tharsus.

▶ *Great views of the city from the Klaipėda Hotel*

She was the subject of an East Prussian love song that was thought to have been composed by Dach. The sculpture was originally crafted by Berlin sculptor Alfred Kune and erected in 1912, but it disappeared during World War II and was never heard of again. The version you see now was recreated in 1989 based on old photos. ⓐ Teatro Aikště

CULTURE

Castle Museum

The port area in which the Castle Museum is located is changing by the day. The museum itself is hidden under a grassy mound but, fortunately, the entrance is well marked. Inside, you can see objects relating to the history of the region from the 16th to 18th centuries. Excavation works are taking place outside, revealing some of the original foundations of the fort. It's possible to wander around and get a sense of history being dug up before your very eyes. ⓐ Pilies 4 🕐 10.00—18.00 Tues—Sun, closed Mon. Admission charge

Witches' Hill

This is where three important Lithuanian traditions come together: wood carving, paganism, and the tendency to act a little bit crazy. The result is the Witches' Hill, or 'Raganų Kalnas'. It consists of a path leading over the wooded dunes and dotted with various strange carved characters with enormous tongues, wild hair, big bulging eyes and all manner of other peculiar features. With the wind whispering through the pines, shadows flitting across the sandy path, and such goggle-eyed ghouls looking at you, it can verge on being a bit creepy.

◀ *Klaipėda's very own guard dog!*

FESTIVAL CITY

The biggest cultural event of the year is the Klaipėda Sea Festival, held in summer each year, generally towards the end of July. For three days the city streets flood with people enjoying concerts, all manner of outdoor eating and drinking venues, stalls, markets, performances and more. If you do want to visit during the Sea Festival, be sure to book accommodation well in advance. Check Ⓦ www.svente.lt for exact dates and a programme of events.

Summer is the time when Klaipėda really comes alive, if in an unpredictable way. Temporary stages pop up in outdoor spaces, particularly in the big apron at the back of the Klaipėda Hotel and on the green triangle of land at the intersection of Tomo and Mėsininkų. You might also come across performances in the grassy area by the lagoon shore in Juodkrantė.

A jazz festival is held every year in early June. See Ⓦ www.jazz.lt

All the statues here were created by local artists and the collection started coming together in 1980. It has grown over the past quarter of a century to become one of the main tourist attractions on the Curonian Spit.

RETAIL THERAPY

Klaipėda is not the finest town for shopping, but it has enough to keep kids amused and you stocked up with supplies. It's best to head for one of the shopping centres.

Akropolis Similar to the Akropolis in Vilnius (see page 96), this recently enlarged shopping centre also boasts cinemas and an ice-skating rink. It makes for a pleasant break from the summer heat. ⓐ Taikos 61 ⓦ www.akropolis.lt

Big The claim that Big is the biggest shopping centre around is a bit dubious, but it's fine for all the usual chains. ⓐ Taikos 139 ⓣ 4636 0773 ⓦ www.big-klaipeda.lt

MegaPlaza Conveniently located in central Klaipėda, this centre contains a dozen or so fashion shops and other chain outlets. ⓐ H Manto 21 ⓦ www.megaplaza.lt

TAKING A BREAK

Boogie Woogie £ Excellent location, churning out cheap and cheery meals to keep the passing crowds happy. ⓐ H Manto 5 ⓣ 4641 1844 ⓛ 11.00–00.00 Mon–Thur, 11.00–02.00 Fri–Sat, 12.00–00.00 Sun

Čili Kaimas £ Tucked under a hideous concrete box of a former cinema is Klaipėda's very own Čili Kaimas restaurant. The recipe here is exactly the same as that used to ensure success in Vilnius (see page 146): efficient service, cheap but good-quality food, and oodles of calories. ⓐ H Manto 11 ⓣ 4631 0953 ⓦ www.cili.lt ⓛ 10.00–00.00 Sun–Thur, 10.00–02.00 Fri & Sat

Senoji Hansa £ This small chain of otherwise unremarkable cafés has one location right near the main square in the Old Town, and is therefore well worth seeking out. In summer, a canopy covers an outdoor seating area which always proves popular – so much so that they can, at times, struggle to provide good service. Food is both cheap and edible, but just relaxing with a drink and a snack seems to be the norm here. ⓐ Kurpių 1 ⓣ 4640 0056 ⓛ 10.00–00.00 Sun–Thur, 11.00–01.30 Fri & Sat

Viskas Lituviškai £ Serving authentic Lithuanian food, this cheap lunch venue is frequented by office workers and manual labourers from the docks alike. The atmosphere is austere, and there probably won't be much English spoken, but it's one of the most authentic experiences you can get in Klaipėda. ⓐ Puodžių 3 ⓣ 4621 6402 ⓛ 10.00–22.00 Mon–Sat, 11.00–22.00 Sun

Navalis £–££ Spilling out from beneath one of the city's smartest hotels is an equally smart café where you can enjoy coffee, croissants, snacks and a spot of people-watching. ⓐ H Manto 23 ⓣ 4640 4200 ⓦ www.navalis.lt ⓛ Café 08.00–00.00, Restaurant 12.00–00.00

Ešerinė ££ If you find yourself somewhere near Nida towards the end of the day, you could do a lot worse than take refuge beneath one of these island-style grass huts and order fish. The food is expensive here, but as is often the case you get what you pay for. Enjoying delicious seafood with such a nice view across the lagoon is a rare pleasure. ⓐ Naglių 2, Nida ⓣ 4695 2757 ⓛ 10.00–00.00

Pašiūrė ££ At first appearance this may look like a grand restaurant, but it's actually a small seasonal affair and the outside seating that you see is all there is to it. Pop in to relax beside the tinkling fountain and be served authentic Lithuanian meals by attractive waitresses in traditional dress. ⓐ Naglių 20, Nida ⓣ 6984 1538 ⓛ 11.00–23.00

◐ *Distinctive wooden architecture in Klaipėda*

AFTER DARK

RESTAURANTS
Memelis ££ An old warehouse facing the river has been turned into a fun-house for grown-ups, with a restaurant and beer hall downstairs and various nightclubs and bars upstairs. The menu focuses on fish

◆ *The popular Memelis brewery and restaurant*

and German-style meals, in keeping with the traditions of the region and the history of the building. The owners brew their own beer downstairs and are happy to serve it in ridiculous portions, including tall four-litre glass tubes with little taps at the bottom. The aim is to set it up on the edge of the table and lie underneath it with your mouth open. One for the boys. ⓐ Žvejų 4 ⓣ 4640 3040 ⓦ www.memelis.lt ⓞ 12.00–00.00 Sun–Thur, 12.00–04.00 Fri & Sat

Skandalas ££–£££ Crammed with corny, American Route-66 kitsch such as number plates, old advertisements and even a bronze Statue of Liberty, this American-style restaurant serves generous, simple and tasty meals. The place buzzes with a fun and friendly crowd at weekends. It's a bit of a stroll away from the centre, but well worth finding. ⓐ Kanto 44 ⓣ 4641 1585 ⓦ www.skandalas.info ⓞ 12.00–01.00 Mon–Thur, 12.00–02.00 Fri & Sat, 12.00–00.00 Sun

BARS & CLUBS

El Calor One of Klaipėda's best Latino clubs, offering dance classes and demonstrations throughout the evening as well as music and dancing. The atmosphere is rather gaudy and the dance floor can get crowded, so watch you don't get pushed down the stairs into the toilets. ⓐ Kepėjų 10 (entrance on Jono) ⓣ 6715 9899 ⓦ www.elcalor.lt ⓞ 22.00–04.00 Wed–Sat, closed Sun–Tues

Eldorado Rather bizarre and occasionally somewhat grim, this fun place has a unique cellar hallway with a stairway entrance at either end. You can go in one end, wander through to see what it's like, and make an easy escape at the other end if you don't like the look of it. ⓐ Lietuvninkų 2 ⓣ 4642 1010 ⓞ 08.30–03.00 Mon–Fri, 10.00–03.00 Sat, 11.00–03.00 Sun

Honolulu A welcome exception to the general standard of nightclub in Klaipėda, Honolulu is clean, safe and welcoming. The over-21 door policy ensures giggly teens stay away and the steep entrance fee is worth it to keep unwanted crowds away from what would otherwise by a cramped interior. The décor is based around an island theme. ⓐ Naujojo Sodo 1 (underneath the Klaipėda Hotel) ⓣ 4640 4372 ⓦ www.klaipedahotel.lt ⓛ 22.30–05.00 Fri & Sat, closed Sun–Thur

Paradox A hotspot for young, often underage clubbers, this rather tacky place has a Russian-kooky feel to it. ⓐ Minijos 2 ⓣ 6877 7001 ⓦ www.clubparadox.lt ⓛ 22.00–05.00 Fri & Sat (hours vary), closed Sun–Thur

Šikšnosparnio Lizdas (Bat's Nest) A hotspot for Goths as well as the curious, this club has a cave-like atmosphere with lots of creative touches, including 'windows' set into each table displaying pieces of old iron gadgets. A fun place to settle in for the evening, although

THE BEST JAZZ CLUB IN LITHUANIA

Kurpiai is often touted as the best jazz club in Lithuania and with good reason. Even when it hasn't attracted the hottest acts, it's a fun place to drop in and spend an evening. There is a wacky layout that makes the place feel that it was just chucked together, and the sort of atmosphere in which people who didn't arrive together nevertheless end up dancing with one another. ⓐ Kurpių 1a ⓣ 4641 0555 ⓦ www.jazz.lt ⓛ 12.00–02.00 Tues–Sat, 12.00–00.00 Sun & Mon

⬥ *Ornate façade in Klaipėda*

you may want to avoid it on a full moon. ⓐ Tiltų 5 ❶ 4631 3412
🕐 11.00–00.00 Mon–Sat, 12.00–00.00 Sun

ACCOMMODATION

Klaipėda Old Town Hostel £ Not actually in the Old Town, but
conveniently right next to the bus station. While things are very
basic here (just a couple of rooms crammed with bunks), it is
a friendly and easy-going place. Take a clothes peg, as there
is a no-shoes policy which has the expected effect in summer.
ⓐ Butkų Juzės 7–4 ❶ 4621 1879 Ⓦ www.lithuanianhostels.org

Astra ££ This hotel is a big white box on the outside, but fluffy and
comfortable on the inside. It is ideally located right next to the ferry
terminal, making it a great base for exploring both Klaipėda and the
Curonian Spit. ⓐ Pilies 2 ❶ 4631 3849 ⓔ hotelastra@takas.lt

Klaipėda Hotel ££ This landmark hotel shows what can be done
with an old Soviet-style tower, plenty of money, and some fancy
interior designers who know what to do with dark wooden panels,
moody lighting and flat-screen televisions. If you can afford it, you
won't regret it. ⓐ Naujojo Sodo 1 ❶ 4640 4372 Ⓦ www.klaipedahotel.lt

Litinterp ££ As is the case in Vilnius and Kaunas, Litinterp in Klaipėda
offers simple, clean and comfortable accommodation at reasonable
prices. The location is excellent given the price, but they can also
organise home stays and accommodation in Nida and Palanga.
ⓐ Puodžių 17 ❶ 4641 0644 Ⓦ www.litinterp.lt

▶ *Railway sign above Vilnius Station tracks*

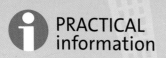

Directory

GETTING THERE

By air

Lithuania is on the budget airline route. **AirBaltic** (Ⓦ www.airbaltic.com) and **flyLAL** (Ⓦ www.lal.lt), formerly Lithuanian Airlines, fly between London Gatwick and Vilnius Airport (see page 50) for reasonable prices. **Ryanair** (Ⓦ www.ryanair.com) flies to Kaunas Airport (see page 50), about 100 km (62 miles) from Vilnius.

Many people are aware that air travel emits CO_2, which contributes to climate change. You may be interested in the possibility of lessening the environmental impact of your flight through Climate Care, which offsets your CO_2 by funding environmental projects around the world. Visit Ⓦ www.climatecare.org

By rail

Trains in Lithuania tend to be slow and uncomfortable. Rail is really only worth considering if you are coming from or going to Russia. A high-speed train line is currently under construction between Vilnius and Kaunas, Lithuania's second largest city, but it is not clear when exactly this will be in operation. See Ⓦ www.litrail.lt for up-to-date information on timetables and routes.

By road

Regular buses ferry travellers between Vilnius and the other Baltic capitals and are ideal for those who are also visiting Latvia or Estonia. Buses are also a good way of travelling to and from cities in Poland and further west. **Eurolines Baltic International** (❶ 5215 1377 Ⓦ www.eurolines.lt) has connections to most European cities including an overnight bus to London.

◓ *Navigate your way around Vilnius*

By sea

Ferries run by **Lisco** (☎ 4639 5051 ⓦ www.lisco.lt) travel to Klaipėda in Lithuania from Kiel and Sassnitz in Germany, Karlshamn in Sweden and Kaliningrad in Russia. **Scandlines** (☎ 4631 0561 ⓦ www.scandlines.lt) operate ferries between Klaipėda and Aabenraa and Arhus in Denmark.

ENTRY FORMALITIES

Lithuania has been a member of the EU since 2004 and a member of the Schengen Agreement since January 1, 2008, so former travelling restrictions have melted away. Citizens of the European Union, United States, Canada, Australia and New Zealand do not require a visa for stays of under three months within a year. Citizens of other countries do require a visa and health insurance. Exact details, including visa application procedures, are on the website of the **Lithuanian Ministry of Foreign Affairs** (ⓦ www.urm.lt).

EU citizens have few incoming customs restrictions except for temporary restrictions sometimes imposed for health and safety reasons. There is a limit of €10,000 in cash. Non-EU citizens are limited to bringing in one litre of spirits or two litres of wine or beer; 200 cigarettes or 100 cigarillos or 50 cigars or 250 g of tobacco. Non EU-citizens are also limited to 50 ml of perfume or 250 ml of eau de toilette.

MONEY

The Lithuanian currency is the litas (Lt), pegged to the euro at an exchange rate of 3.45Lt to €1. The rule of thumb for UK travellers is 5 litas to the pound. Lithuania is expected to be ready to adopt the euro sometime after 2010. Euros are not widely accepted, except for in a handful of shops in the centre. Sterling and US dollars are not accepted at all. Currency can be changed at bureaux de change at the airport and train stations as well as many locations in the Old Town, including casinos.

The easiest way to withdraw money is through an ATM machine. ATMs are abundant in Vilnius, including at the airport, bus and train stations, but can be less common in smaller villages. Take plenty of cash if you are planning an out-of-town adventure.

Credit cards (MasterCard and Visa) are widely accepted in larger stores, but be aware that smaller or new businesses will often only accept cash.

HEALTH, SAFETY & CRIME

Tap water is perfectly safe to drink in Vilnius, although most locals prefer bottled water. The standard of public healthcare is improving but hospital facilities may not appear to be up to Western standards and tend to suffer from corruption. Bring a European Health Insurance Card (EHIC Ⓦ www.ehic.org.uk) for free or reduced-cost treatment in public clinics and hospitals. Private clinics abound, catering to a growing stream of health tourists from the UK who come here for operations, and the quality of service they provide is often world-class. See page 154 for more details.

Police in Lithuania are fairly stern and not generally helpful to tourists who ask the time or for directions. They should, however, be your first point of contact if you are the victim of theft or violence. They are dressed in green and always work in pairs, one of whom is supposed to speak English. While this is rarely the case in reality, the situation is improving.

Vilnius Old Town is generally a very safe place to visit and pickpocketing is not as common here as it is in most European cities these days. As usual, however, you should exercise caution by sticking to well-lit streets in the Old Town at night and by keeping a sharp eye out for potential problems, including keeping your drink with you at all times. Leave valuables safely locked up at your hotel and avoid any late-night invitations to someone's home.

Lithuanians have a reputation for being racist, and although this is not true for all locals there are sometimes cases of dark-skinned visitors being turned away from nightclubs.

However you book your city break, it is important to take out adequate personal travel insurance for the trip. For peace of mind the policy should give cover for medical expenses, loss, theft, repatriation, personal liability and cancellation expenses. If you are travelling in your own vehicle you should also check that you are appropriately insured. Make sure you take relevant insurance documents and your driving licence with you and leave photocopies of them in a safe place.

OPENING HOURS

Opening hours can vary wildly in Lithuania, particularly in more rural areas. Standard business hours are from 09.00–18.00 and restaurants are generally open 12.00–00.00. Grocery stores and supermarkets are mostly open 07.00–22.00 daily.

Nightlife happens late – many nightclubs might not even open until 22.00 and don't get going until midnight. At weekends nightclubs close at about 05.00, and then many people simply head to one of the all-night cafés or bars. Vilnius is a city that doesn't encourage sleep.

Opening hours are usually printed on the doors of shops and restaurants, sometimes as a line of blocks or Roman numerals, one representing each day of the week from Monday (I) to Sunday (VII).

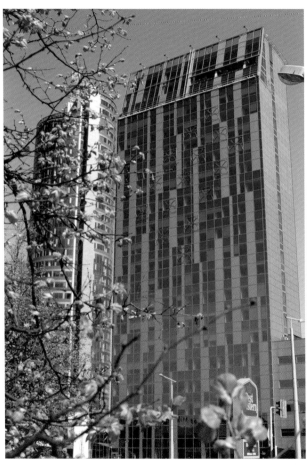

○ *Vilnius government building*

TOILETS

The horrors of squatting have ceased. These days you'd have to go out of your way to find an old-fashioned Soviet-era toilet. Clean public toilets charging a small fee are scattered around a few parks and streets in the city. If there's not one nearby, the best option is to head into a café or hotel foyer and – if you have no intention of buying a coffee or becoming a customer – asking politely.

Be careful of the gender signs. The gents is marked with a triangle which is broad at the top and pointed at the bottom (think 'broad shoulders') while the ladies is the other way round (think 'skirt'). You might also see 'V' for men (*vyrai*) and 'M' for women (*moterys*). The international 'WC' is used to signpost toilets.

CHILDREN

Children will be welcome in Vilnius as much as in any Western city. There are children's play areas in the parks, but you should be aware that the equipment in them is not as well maintained as you might like. There are no health-and-safety watchdogs here.

It's not common to find baby-change facilities or high chairs in shops, cafés or restaurants. Nappies and other baby supplies, however, are all available in supermarkets (see page 26).

An ideal day out for older kids is a trip to the Akropolis shopping and entertainment centre (see page 96). It's home to a handy ice-skating rink, as well as cinemas, plenty of restaurants, and of course shops. Films are generally shown in the original language with Lithuanian subtitles, but do check before buying a ticket.

For a restaurant with a child-friendly twist, try **Čili Kaimas** (ⓐ Vokiečių 8 ⓣ 5231 2536 ⓦ www.cili.lt ⓛ 10.00–00.00 Sun–Thur,

● *Higher Castle can easily be reached by funicular railway*

⬤ *Traditional Russian dolls can be found on market stalls*

10.00–02.00 Fri & Sat). Downstairs, there's a large pool stocked with fish which will keep kids amused for hours, as will the live chickens near the entrance upstairs and the grass snake near the toilets. There's also a *babushka* – a Russian-style 'grandmother' who rattles out stories – and other theatrical entertainment for kids from 12.00 to 14.00 on Sundays. Unfortunately it's in Lithuanian only, but it might provide some distraction for the kids while you have a meal.

Another family-friendly restaurant is **Marceliukės Klėtis** (ⓐ Tuskulenu 3S ① 5272 5087 ① 11.00–00.00 Tues–Sat, 11.00–23.00 Sun & Mon), located amid car parks and flats adjacent to Kalvarių Market – see the north-east corner of the map on page 93. It's a short taxi ride, but you can also get trolleybus 5 or 6 from outside the Novotel hotel. Upstairs is a dining room surrounded by a miniature adventure playground, with a cubby house to explore, lots of mysterious passageways and stairways, and a big slide made from what looks like a fallen log. There's even a low table with child-sized seats, in case they do actually want to sit down and eat. For family-friendly fun, this place is highly recommended, and it's also a decent place to try traditional Lithuanian food.

COMMUNICATIONS
Internet
Most of the Old Town is covered by pay-as-you-go Wi-Fi. You can wander into most cafés and restaurants in the main tourist areas with a laptop and expect to be connected. Some cafés and restaurants offer free Wi-Fi. In both cases, the signal strength and connection speeds are usually excellent.

If you don't have your own computer, you can get on the internet for free at Mano Kavinė (see page 73), where they will happily let you sip and surf using the computer at the bar. There are a few internet cafés scattered about the city but the best is **Collegium** (ⓔ Pilies 22), entered through an archway on the left-hand side of a little courtyard.

Phone

Public telephones operate on a card system. You can pick up cards from post offices and kiosks marked *Lietuvos Spauda*. Paying for the call is the easy part. Working out Lithuania's baffling array of prefixes is the hurdle.

TELEPHONING VILNIUS

The country code for Lithuania is 370 and the area code for Vilnius is 5. Basic telephone numbers have seven digits. If you see a seven-digit Vilnius phone number, you can call it from abroad by dialling 00 370 5 followed by the number.

Note that every phone number in Lithuania is prefixed with an 8 – but only if you're dialling from a mobile phone or from a different city within Lithuania and are not using the international format. To dial Vilnius from Kaunas, for instance, you would dial 8, then 5, then the seven-digit number. To be safe, simply use the international format for all calls you make.

TELEPHONING ABROAD

To make an international call from within Lithuania, dial 00 followed by the country code for the destination country, such as 44 for the UK, 1 for the US and Canada, or 61 for Australia. This is followed by the area code (usually omitting the first '0' if there is one) and the number you require.

If you need helping using the phones contact the national telephone company **TEO** (☎ 117 from within Vilnius, or ☎ 370 8000 0117 from elsewhere Ⓦ www.teo.lt).

Post

The postal service in Lithuania is generally very good, although service can be rather abrupt in post offices, where queuing systems for different services are strict and waits can be long. Mail can go missing, so if you want to be sure your letter will arrive, use the registered postal service. Standard rates for postcards are 1.55Lt within Lithuania, 2.45Lt within the EU, and 2.90Lt outside the EU but be aware that letters tend to weigh and cost more. See Ⓦ www.post.lt for more detailed information.

ELECTRICITY

Lithuania runs on 240 volts using European-style two-pin sockets. Buy adaptors before you come as they are not readily available in the main tourist area. If you do need to buy an adaptor, head for the Akropolis shopping centre (see page 96) where you will find an 'Elektromarkt' store.

TRAVELLERS WITH DISABILITIES

Vilnius wasn't designed for wheelchair users or people with other disabilities but the city is making efforts to better the situation and things are improving rapidly. There are now plenty of wheelchair-friendly venues but the trouble rests in getting there. The cobbled streets, narrow pavements and abundance of stairs make it difficult for those with wheelchairs or mobility difficulties to get around.

The newer buses and trolleybuses now have low-entry doors and space inside for wheelchairs. These are gradually replacing

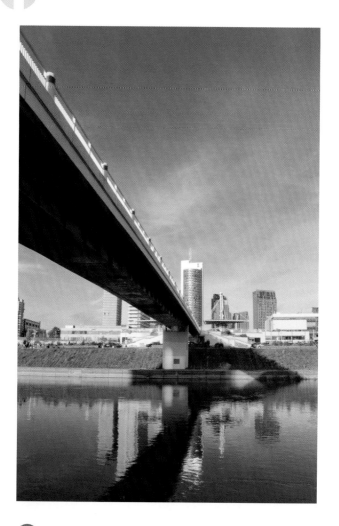

the older fleet of groaning and lumbering vehicles which are not recommended for their ease of access. For specific, up-to-date information and advice contact the **Lithuanian Council for Disabled Affairs** (ⓐ Vaidilutės 69 ❶ 5231 6649).

TOURIST INFORMATION

Tourist information offices are located at:

Central ⓐ Vilniaus 22 ❶ 5262 9660

Town Hall ⓐ Didžioji 31 ❶ 5262 6470

Railway station ⓐ Geležinkelio 16 ❶ 5269 2091

Their website (ⓦ www.turizmas.vilnius.lt) is not always up to date but the staff at the tourist information offices are generally multilingual, pleasant and helpful.

Those visiting Vilnius with an interest in Jewish history and culture should drop into the **Jewish Community Centre** (ⓐ Pylimo 4 ❶ 5261 3003) or the new **Jewish Cultural and Information Centre** (ⓐ Mėsinių 3a/5 ❶ 5261 6422).

BACKGROUND READING

Vilnius In Your Pocket is published every two months and is good for up-to-date listings information and reviews. Find it in bookstores, tourist information centres and kiosks.

Vilnius City Guide by Tomas Venclova provides an excellent overview of the city and its history, in a format that is small enough to stick in your bag and carry around as you explore.

Literary books and novels by Lithuanian authors are rarely available in English translation.

◀ *A bridge crosses the river and leads to modern Vilnius*

Emergencies

112 is the all-purpose emergency number. It works from any fixed or mobile phone in Lithuania. It should be used for all and any genuine emergencies, including police, ambulance and fire. Lithuania does not have a system in place to locate the source of your call, so be prepared to give address details.

Emergencies of the 'chocolate and flowers at midnight' variety are best dealt with by calling the **general information hotline** (☎ 118 or 1588), for which you will pay a small fee.

If you break down while driving anywhere in Lithuania, call **Altas Assistance** (☎ 8 800 181 00 from a fixed-line phone or 1810 from a local mobile). In Vilnius, they have a basic 35Lt call-out fee plus the cost of any work done. Out of town, expect to pay 75Lt for the call-out.

MEDICAL SERVICES

The main public hospital is the **Vilnius University Emergency Hospital** (☎ Šiltnamių 29 ☎ 5216 9140).

There are several private hospitals with English-speaking staff that offer 24-hour emergency care. These include: **Baltic American Medical & Surgical Clinic** (☎ Nemenčinės 54a ☎ 5234 2020) and the **Medical Diagnostic Centre** (☎ V Grybo 32/10 ☎ 5270 9120).

For general medical help during business hours, the most central and convenient option is the **Med General Private Clinic** (☎ Gedimino 1a/19, 2nd floor ☎ 5261 3534). Pharmacies (*vaistin*) are plentiful.

For dental help, contact **Stomatologijos Klinika** (☎ Labdarių 7/11 ☎ 5261 9623).

EMERGENCY PHRASES

Help!	**Fire!**	**Stop!**
Padėkite!	Gaisras!	Stop!
Pah-deck-it-eh!	*Ghays-rus!*	*Stop!*

Call an ambulance/a doctor/ the police/the fire brigade!
Iškvieskite greitąjà pagalbà/gydytojà/policijà/gaisrininkus!
Ish-ques-kee-teh gray-tah-yah pah-gull-bah/ghee-dee-toh-yah/poh-lee-tsee-yah/ghay-sree-neen-coos!

POLICE

The main police station (🅐 Saltoniškių 19, room 107 🕙 08.00–12.00 & 12.45–17.00 Mon–Thur, 08.00–12.00 & 12.45–16.45 Fri) is located some way out of the city centre.

However, this is just an administrative office and it is unlikely that anyone there would speak English. If you need assistance from the police you should always call them by telephone using the emergency number 🕿 112

EMBASSIES & CONSULATES

Australia 🅐 Vilniaus 23 🕿 5212 3369
Canada 🅐 Jogailos 4 🕿 5249 0950
Republic of Ireland 🅐 Jogailos 4 🕿 5269 0044
UK 🅐 Antakalnio 2 🕿 5246 2900
USA 🅐 Akmenų 6 🕿 5266 5500

WHAT'S IN YOUR GUIDEBOOK?

Independent authors Impartial up-to-date information from our travel experts who meticulously source local knowledge.

Experience Thomas Cook's 165 years in the travel industry and guidebook publishing enriches every word with expertise you can trust.

Travel know-how Contributions by thousands of staff around the globe, each one living and breathing travel.

Editors Travel-publishing professionals, pulling everything together to craft a perfect blend of words, pictures, maps and design.

You, the traveller We deliver a practical, no-nonsense approach to information, geared to how you really use it.

Editorial/project management: Lisa Plumridge with Laetitia Clapton
Copy editor: Monica Guy
Layout/DTP: Alison Rayner
Proofreader: Wendy Janes

SPOTTED YOUR NEXT CITY BREAK?

Then these lightweight CitySpots pocket guides will have you in the know in no time, wherever you're heading. Covering over 80 cities worldwide, they're packed with detail on the most important urban attractions from shopping and sights to non-stop nightlife; knocking spots off chunkier, clunkier versions.

Aarhus	Genoa	Paris
Amsterdam	Glasgow	Prague
Antwerp	Gothenburg	Porto
Athens	Granada	Reykjavik
Bangkok	Hamburg	Riga
Barcelona	Hanover	Rome
Belfast	Helsinki	Rotterdam
Belgrade	Hong Kong	Salzburg
Berlin	Istanbul	Sarajevo
Bilbao	Kiev	Seville
Bologna	Krakow	Singapore
Bordeaux	Kuala Lumpur	Sofia
Bratislava	Leipzig	Stockholm
Bruges	Lille	Strasbourg
Brussels	Lisbon	St Petersburg
Bucharest	Ljubljana	Tallinn
Budapest	London	Tirana
Cairo	Los Angeles	Tokyo
Cape Town	Lyon	Toulouse
Cardiff	Madrid	Turin
Cologne	Marrakech	Valencia
Copenhagen	Marseilles	Venice
Cork	Milan	Verona
Dubai	Monte Carlo	Vienna
Dublin	Moscow	Vilnius
Dubrovnik	Munich	Warsaw
Düsseldorf	Naples	Zagreb
Edinburgh	New York	Zurich
Florence	Nice	
Frankfurt	Oslo	
Gdansk	Palermo	
Geneva	Palma	

Available from all good bookshops, your local Thomas Cook travel store or browse and buy on-line at www.thomascookpublishing.com

The publishers would like to thank the following individuals and organisations for supplying their copyright photographs for this book: Lars Bryne, page 77; Dreamstime.com (Marc Johnson, pages 23 & 139; Asta Plechavičiūtė, page 5; Regimantas Ramanauskas, pages 42–3 & 152), elianadulins/iStockphoto.com, page 47; Druskininkai Tourist Information, pages 113 & 118; Klaipėda City Municipality, page 115; Pictures Colour Library, page 148; Andrew Quested, pages 9, 11, 15, 19, 22, 26, 35, 37, 49, 51, 58, 61, 67, 69, 71, 81, 84, 87, 88, 97, 105, 107, 127, 133, 134 & 141; Richard Schofield, pages 121, 123 & 128; SXC.hu (Robert J, page 101; Domantas Jankauskas, page 108); Tourism Division of Vilnius City Municipal Government, pages 7, 12, 21, 25, 29, 45, 65, 94, 99, 111, 117, 145 & 147; Ray Vysniauskas, pages 33 & 38.

Send your thoughts to
books@thomascook.com

- Found a great bar, club, shop or must-see sight that we don't feature?
- Like to tip us off about any information that needs a little updating?
- Want to tell us what you love about this handy little guidebook and more importantly how we can make it even handier?

Then here's your chance to tell all! Send us ideas, discoveries and recommendations today and then look out for your valuable input in the next edition of this title.

Email the above address (stating the title) or write to:
CitySpots Project Editor, Thomas Cook Publishing, PO Box 227, Coningsby Road, Peterborough PE3 8SB, UK.